West Academic Publishing's Law School Advisory Board

a short & happy guide to

Securities Regulation

Jennifer O'Hare
The Martin G. McGuinn Chair in Business Law and Professor of Law
Villanova University Charles Widger School of Law

A SHORT & HAPPY GUIDE® SERIES

WEST ACADEMIC

860 Blue Gentian Road, Suite 350
Eagan, MN 55121
1-877-888-1330

Published in the United States of America

ISBN: 978-1-68467-229-5

Acknowledgments

Thanks to my family, for their constant love and support. They make me happy every day!

Thanks to Ann Juliano, a two-time "Short & Happy Guide" author, who encouraged me to take on this project.

And thanks to my students—past and present—who've helped me gain a better understanding of securities regulation and become a better teacher.

Table of Contents

A Short & Happy Guide to Securities Regulation

CHAPTER 1

Introduction to Securities Regulation

A. What Is "Securities Regulation?"

What is "securities regulation?" When I registered for the class back in law school, I didn't know what it was, either. All I knew was that attorneys at my future law firm suggested I take the class. So I did. But, candidly, even after the semester ended, I still didn't really understand securities regulation. The material was complex, the statutes were hard to read, and even though I put a lot of time into preparing for class, it just wasn't clicking for me. Hopefully, this book can help make it click for you.

Basically, securities regulation refers to two federal statutes: the Securities Act of 1933 and the Securities Exchange Act of 1934. The '33 Act regulates the sale of securities from an issuer, such as corporation, to investors. In other words, when a company wants to raise money by selling stock, it must comply with the '33 Act. The '34 Act regulates what happens after the securities are sold to investors. Among other things, the '34 Act oversees the trading markets and requires public companies to provide information to investors.

It may surprise you to learn that there was no federal regulation of securities until 1933. Everything worked relatively smoothly for over 150 years, until it didn't—which led to the Great Depression of 1929. Following the market crash, Congress heard testimony from lots of angry investors who complained that they had purchased stock that turned out to be worthless. Often these investors had been given no information about the securities they purchased, or, if they had been given information, the information wasn't true.

Congress had an important regulatory choice to make: it could regulate the merits of securities offerings or regulate the disclosures made in securities offerings. Merit regulation would have given the government the power to stop a company from selling securities that the government considered to be too risky or dangerous. Congress decided against that approach. Instead, Congress decided on mandatory disclosure. The idea is to let investors make their own decisions, but to make sure they're informed decisions. This remains the approach to securities regulation to this day.

B. It's All About Disclosure

Disclosure is the foundation of the '33 and the '34 Acts. This is one of the keys to understanding the Securities Regulation class. The federal securities laws seek to ensure that investors have the information they need to make informed investment decisions. Thus, for example, when a company sells securities to the public, it must provide a disclosure document in the form of a Registration Statement to help potential investors make an informed decision on whether to purchase the securities. And when a publicly traded company asks its shareholders to vote at the annual meeting, it must provide a disclosure document in the form of a Proxy Statement to help them make an informed voting decision. Moreover, throughout the year, publicly traded companies must provide periodic reports to help investors make informed decisions on whether they should keep or trade their securities.

The federal government—mostly through the Securities and Exchange Commission—decides what disclosure must be provided, when disclosure must be provided, how the disclosure must be provided, and who must be provided with the disclosure. In general, the SEC makes these decisions by balancing two important, but often competing, policy considerations: (1) protecting investors; and (2) promoting efficiency, competition, and capital formation.

The goal of investor protection is met through meaningful mandatory disclosure. Presumably, the more disclosure, the greater the investor protection. But disclosure comes at a cost—not to investors, who get it for free, but to the companies that are forced to provide it. And it's not cheap. First, the information must be generated. Then lawyers must ensure the disclosures meet the requirements of the federal securities laws. Companies must also retain third parties (such as accountants) to check certain disclosures, including the company's financial statements. There are printing and mailing expenses. In addition, there are other types of costs associated with mandatory disclosure. For example, the company is forced to share information with its competitors, which may harm its business. Finally, mandatory disclosure opens the company up to securities fraud class actions, which impose additional costs on the company.

These costs are a drag on a company's financial results. If the costs get too high, companies could decide not to go public, which cuts them off from capital that could help grow the company. That's not a good thing for the company or for the U.S. economy. Similarly, companies that are already publicly traded may choose to "go private" to avoid the on-going costs of mandatory disclosure. Once again, this is not a good thing for the efficiency and competitiveness of U.S. markets.

The SEC, therefore, must decide whether the benefits of mandatory disclosure exceed the costs. In making this decision, the SEC has a lot to consider. For example, who are the investors? Are they sophisticated market professionals who can take care of themselves? If so, maybe they don't need the protections of mandatory disclosure. On the other hand, if the investors are "ordinary" people saving for retirement, they may need more information to understand their investments. If so, what information? And how much information? Is there such a thing as too much information?

Similarly, should all companies provide the same information? Perhaps smaller companies that aren't followed by many analysts should be required to disclose more information than large, more established companies that are well-known to the investing public. Similarly, maybe larger companies should be required to disclose less information to the investing public. But what about the costs of disclosure? If it's too expensive for some companies to disclose the information, what should be done?

And what about the role of technology? Things have changed a lot since 1933, when disclosure could be made only through written documents delivered by mail. Should companies be able to make disclosure through postings on corporate websites or through social media? These approaches are cheaper, but are they as effective?

This is why so many of the securities rules seem so complicated. The SEC is trying its best to balance these two competing policy interests. To do a good job, the rules often include exceptions, exemptions, and exclusions. If you can remember the two policy considerations underlying the rules, you'll probably find it easier to understand the rules. Or, at the very least, you won't feel that the rules are simply an evil trap set by the SEC for unwary 2L and 3L law students.

C. It's Also About Securities Fraud

No matter how much disclosure is required, it won't protect investors if it's not true. That's why the securities laws also include numerous anti-fraud provisions. Under the federal securities laws, outright lies are illegal, and so are misleading statements or half-truths.

As we'll see later in this book, securities fraud claims are usually brought by investors as class actions. Class actions often occur in situations where a lot of people have been harmed by a particular act, but each person suffers only minimal damages. This is what happens when a publicly traded company makes a false or misleading statement. Hundreds of thousands of investors may be hurt, but the damages may just a few dollars per share of stock.

In situations like this, it's unlikely that anyone would bother to sue because the costs of bringing the action would exceed any recovered damages. The legal system recognized this problem a long time ago. To address it, equity courts invented the "class action," which allows a representative to sue on behalf of all of the people who had been harmed.

Securities class actions are controversial. On the one hand, supporters point out that without class actions, investors wouldn't get any compensation for their losses. In addition, they argue that class actions deter securities fraud. The SEC doesn't have the resources to sue every company that commits securities fraud. Private actions can help fill this gap, and companies know it. On the other hand, critics argue that most securities class actions are frivolous and that they're brought by lawyers when there is no evidence of fraud, only an unexplained drop in stock price. According to this argument, the lawyers are just looking for a settlement, and the company will pay the settlement to make the nuisance case go away. Investors receive very little from the settlements, but the lawyers representing the investors take 30% or more off the top of the settlement. Moreover, since insurance companies, not the wrongdoers, pay the settlements, class actions don't actually deter wrongful conduct. Both sides have valid points.

To understand the securities fraud section of the Securities Regulation class, you need to recognize that this "securities fraud class actions are good" v. "securities fraud class actions are bad" debate is always going on in the background. Congress and the courts are trying to find a way to determine whether the securities fraud case is frivolous or not, and they've each developed rules to help sort the cases. Sometimes, we're in a "pro-plaintiff" environment, and sometimes we're in a "pro-defendant" environment. Recognizing this will help you understand securities fraud.

D. And Don't Forget "Materiality"

"Materiality" is a concept that runs throughout the federal securities laws. Sometimes, the federal securities laws require disclosure of information only if it is "material." Put another way, if the information isn't material, the company won't have to disclose it. Materiality is also a fundamental part of securities fraud. That's because the federal securities laws don't prohibit all false or misleading statements of fact; they prohibit false or misleading statements of *material* fact. Thus, in many securities fraud cases, the parties are arguing about whether the company's statement was material.

The good news is that there is a settled definition of materiality. According to the U.S. Supreme Court, information is a material if "there is a substantial likelihood that a reasonable shareholder would consider it important in deciding how to [act]." *See* TSC Industries, Inc. v. Northway, Inc., 426 U.S. 438 (1976). The bad news is that this definition can be difficult to apply. We'll work on it later in this book in Chapter 11.

E. The Role of the SEC

Your professor probably assigned a statutory supplement for your class. Take a look at it. The '33 Act and the '34 Act are only a small part of it. As you can see, most of securities regulation is found in the rules. What's the difference? Statutes are enacted by Congress, while rules are promulgated by the SEC. You may think that rules are less important than statutes, but they're not. SEC rules are equally as important as the statutes.

Soon after passing the '33 Act, Congress realized that it needed help to oversee the federal securities laws. The next year, as part of the '34 Act, Congress created the Securities and Exchange Commission. The SEC is a federal agency headed by five Commissioners who are appointed by the President and confirmed by the Senate. One of these Commissioners is selected by the President to be the Chairperson of the SEC. Each Commissioner serves a staggered five-year term.

The SEC is an independent agency, which means that the SEC doesn't report to the President. The President can't fire a Commissioner for not sharing the President's viewpoints or policies. Instead, the President can only remove a Commissioner for cause. In addition, no more than three Commissioners can be members of the same political party. These structures were intended to give the Commissioners the freedom to uphold the mission of the SEC without political pressure.

However, the composition of the Commission certainly makes a difference in the SEC's agenda. When a Democrat is in the White House, the SEC is usually seen as more interested in promoting the first policy underlying the federal securities laws—investor protection. When a Republican is President, the SEC is usually viewed as more concerned about the second policy—facilitating efficient markets, competition, and capital formation.

Congress has delegated a tremendous amount of authority to the SEC. To meet their responsibilities, the Commissioners get help from SEC staff, who work in one of the SEC's six divisions, 14 offices, or 11 regional offices. For Securities Regulation students, the most important division is probably Corporation Finance. "Corp Fin" recommends new mandatory disclosure rules and amendments to existing rules to the Commissioners. It creates the "forms" that are used to make mandatory disclosure. It reviews the mandatory disclosure documents filed with the SEC. Basically, Corp Fin is charged with making sure that investors have the information they need to make informed investment decisions. We'll see Corp Fin's work throughout this book.

F. Other Helpful Things You Should Know

Just a few more things before we get started. First, securities lawyers refer to the statutes as the '33 Act (or the Securities Act) and the '34 Act (or the Exchange Act). We do the same thing for the rules. In other words, we don't refer to the U.S. Code or the Code of Federal Regulations. But once in a while you might see citations to the U.S.C. or the CFR. In case you do, here's the translation:

Securities Act of 1933	15 U.S.C. §§ 77a-77aa
Securities Exchange Act of 1934	15 U.S.C. §§ 78a-78rr
'33 Act Rules	17 C.F.R. Part 230
'34 Act Rules	17 C.F.R. Part 240

In addition, securities lawyers sometimes refer to the Congressional acts that amended the federal securities laws. In other words, lawyers may talk about the Sarbanes-Oxley Act or the Williams Act. It's essentially a shorthand way to refer to the amendments to the securities laws that were made in those acts.

Here's a short description of the amendments made in some of the more important acts:

The Williams Act (1968)	Amended the federal securities laws to regulate corporate takeovers
The Private Securities Litigation Reform Act (1995)	Amended the federal securities laws to reduce frivolous securities fraud class actions
The Securities Litigation Uniform Standards Act (1998)	Amended the federal securities laws to preempt state securities fraud class actions
Sarbanes-Oxley Act (2002)	Amended the federal securities laws to improve the quality of financial statements and financial reporting
Dodd-Frank Wall Street Reform and Consumer Protection Act (2010)	Amended the federal securities laws to reform the financial system and reduce the risk of a future financial crisis
Jumpstart Our Business Startups Act (2012)	Amended the federal securities laws to reduce the regulatory burden on small businesses looking to raise capital

So, that's it for the introduction. Let's get started.

CHAPTER 2

What Is a "Security?"

A. Introduction

Have you noticed that pretty much every Securities Regulation casebook or study aid starts with the definition of "security?" I'm sorry to be following the crowd. But it makes sense because for the securities laws to apply, the transaction must involve a "security." It's the gateway to the federal securities laws.

The '33 Act and the '34 Act each include definition sections, and the term "security" is defined similarly in each act. The '33 Act provides that:

> The term "security" means any note, stock, treasury stock, security future, security-based swap, bond, debenture, evidence of indebtedness, certificate of interest or participation in any profit-sharing agreement, collateral-trust certificate, preorganization certificate or subscription, transferable share, investment contract, voting-trust certificate, certificate of deposit for a security, fractional undivided interest in oil, gas, or other mineral rights, any put, call, straddle, option, or privilege on any security, certificate of deposit, or group or index of securities (including any

> interest therein or based on the value thereof), or any put, call, straddle, option, or privilege entered into on a national securities exchange relating to foreign currency, or, in general, any interest or instrument commonly known as a "security", or any certificate of interest or participation in, temporary or interim certificate for, receipt for, guarantee of, or warrant or right to subscribe to or purchase, any of the foregoing.

See Securities Act of 1933§ 2(1).

As you can see, this "definition" isn't much of a definition at all. It merely sets forth a long list of instruments that have been commonly understood to be securities—like stock, promissory notes, and a variety of derivatives. Securities lawyers often refer to this list as "enumerated securities." Most people would agree that these instruments—which are commonly understood to be investment vehicles—should be regulated by the federal securities laws.

But what about ventures that don't fall into one of these enumerated securities? Are they securities? The answer depends on whether they are "investment contracts."

B. Investment Contracts

Take another look at the definition of security. In the fourth line, sandwiched between "transferable share" and "voting trust certificate" is the term "investment contract." These two little words have dramatically expanded the definition of security. It's how the federal securities laws regulate the sale of non-traditional investments, such as sales of interests in a chinchilla ranch or an earthworm farm.

"Investment contract" was defined by the U.S. Supreme Court in the *Howey* case. *See* SEC v. W.J. Howey Co., 328 U.S. 293 (1946). In that case, Howey sold narrow strips of land in an orange grove primarily to tourists visiting Florida. Because the purchasers wouldn't be able to take care of the orange trees on their specific strips, Howey also offered each purchaser a service agreement, under which Howey agreed to cultivate the orange trees, harvest the oranges, and distribute the profits from the orange sales to the purchasers based on a percentage of the orange grove each purchaser owned.

The SEC brought an action against Howey, contending that Howey should have registered the sales under the federal securities laws. The SEC and Howey had very different ideas about what Howey had sold. According to Howey, it had sold real property. According to the SEC, Howey had sold a security. The SEC argued that the sale of real property coupled with the service agreement created an investment contract. The Supreme Court agreed.

In reaching that conclusion, the Supreme Court defined investment contract as a transaction in which:

(1) a person invests money or property

(2) in a common enterprise

(3) and is led to expect profits

(4) primarily from the efforts of others.

If all four prongs are met, voila! An investment contract has been created, and the federal securities laws are implicated.

Let's dig a little deeper into each prong.

1. Investment of Money

Under the investment prong, the key is to identify the buyer's motivation for making the payment to a third party. Ask yourself, why did the buyer give money to a third person? It's not always to invest. Often, it's to obtain something to use or to consume. In *Howey*, however, the investment motivation was clear. The individuals who purchased the units in the orange grove did so to earn profits when the oranges were later harvested and sold. The purchasers weren't intending to eat any oranges that were grown on their strip of land.

To use another example . . . let's assume that I paid $500,000 for a condo in a luxury beach development that'll serve as my primary residence. Did I "invest" money? No, my motivation was to have a place to live—a consumption motivation, not an investment motivation. Thus, the first *Howey* prong isn't met. On the other hand, what if I purchased the condo with the idea of renting it to other people? Did I "invest" money? Yes, my motivation was to receive profits in the form of monthly rental payments. Thus, the first *Howey* prong would be met.

2. Common Enterprise

The Supreme Court didn't provide much analysis of common enterprise in the *Howey* case, but the definition of "common" means something shared by two or more individuals. In *Howey*, the common enterprise element was met because each investor pooled their money in the venture, meaning that the risks of the venture were *shared by the investors* in accordance with the amount of their investment. In other words, if I owned 10% of the orange grove, I would receive 10% of any profits. This is an example of *horizontal commonality*. It's called "horizontal" because the commonality is tested between the investors, who are depicted horizontally in the following graphic:

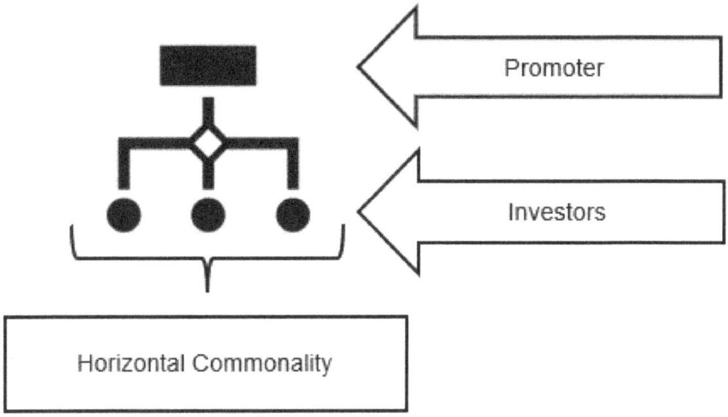

Some lower courts have created another way to meet the common enterprise prong: *vertical commonality*. While horizontal commonality focuses on the relationship between the investors, vertical commonality focuses on the relationship between each investor and the *promoter*—hence, the following graphic:

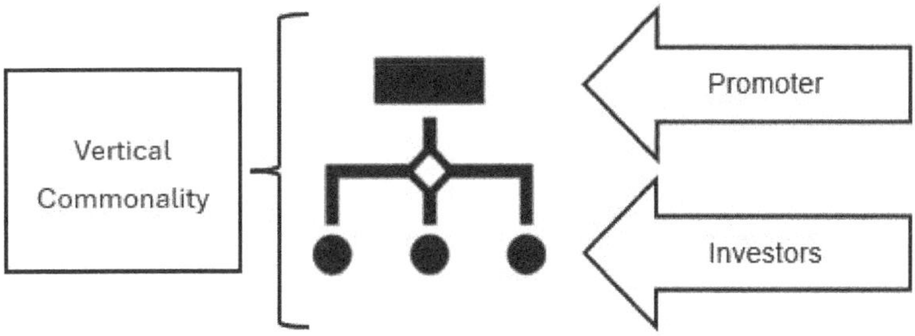

Why did these lower courts create vertical commonality? To prevent sketchy promoters from getting around the federal securities laws by marketing non-traditional investments to only one investor. If there's only one investor, there can be no pooling, which means no horizontal commonality, which means no investment contract, which means no regulation of the sale of the non-traditional investment. Because vertical commonality tests the common enterprise between the promoter and each individual investor, vertical commonality can be found even if there is only one investor.

Here's where it starts to get complicated (if it hasn't already). Lower courts have recognized two types of vertical commonality: (1) strict vertical commonality; and (2) broad vertical commonality. *Strict vertical commonality* requires the promoter and the investor to share the risks of the venture. There must be a connection between the *success* of the promoter and *success* of the investor. In other words, if there is strict vertical commonality, the promoter won't get a return unless the investor also gets a return. *Broad vertical commonality*, on the other hand, merely requires a connection between the *efforts* of promoter and the *success* of the investor. This means that the promoter and the investor don't have to share the risk of the venture. With broad vertical commonality, the promoter can make a profit, even if the investor doesn't.

Let's use my beach condo purchase to illustrate the difference between strict and broad vertical commonality. When I purchased that beach condo, let's assume that the developer also offered to help me rent it out. Under this arrangement, the developer agreed to market my condo to renters, keep it clean, deal with renters and payments, and distribute the rental payments to me. In return, the developer would receive a monthly payment of $100.

Here, broad vertical commonality exists. If the developer doesn't do its job, I won't receive any profits. Therefore, there's a connection between the *efforts* of the developer and my *success* as the investor. Notice, however, that the developer will receive a $100 fee each month, regardless of whether my condo is rented out—so there is no risk sharing between us. That's okay under broad vertical commonality.

But it's not okay under strict vertical commonality. Remember that strict vertical commonality requires sharing of risks. There must be a connection between the *success* of the promoter and the *success* of the investor. An example of this would be if the fee structure provided that the developer would receive 10% of any revenue generated by renting my condo. Since the promoter gets paid only if I get paid, the strict vertical commonality element is met.

3. Led to Expect Profits

In general, this prong isn't hard to meet. Look for facts that show that the promoter was marketing the venture as an investment. For example, in *Howey*, the developer pitched the venture as an investment, projecting 10-20% returns.

Similarly, it's generally easy to show "profits." Profits include dividends, an increase in the value of the investment, and interest payments—pretty much any financial return to the investor will constitute a profit.

4. Primarily from the Efforts of Others

The "primarily from the efforts of others" prong requires that the "essential managerial efforts which affect the failure or success of the enterprise" are made by someone other than the investor. *See* SEC v. Glenn W. Turner Enters., 474 F.2d 476, 482-3 (9th Cir. 1973), cert. denied, 414 U.S. 821(1973). In other words, for an investment contract to exist, the investor must be largely passive. Given the federal securities laws emphasis on disclosure, the emphasis on passivity makes sense. If an investor relies on a promoter for returns, the investor's need for information becomes more important.

With this prong, there are two issues to keep an eye on. The first occurs when the investor isn't entirely passive. If the investor is working in the venture, then profits could be attributable to the investor's efforts, and not the promoter's efforts. Some investor involvement is okay, but too much involvement will negate the "primarily from the efforts of others" prong—meaning no investment contract. We'll talk more about this below, in our discussion of whether partnership interests are investment contracts.

The second issue arises if the profits aren't due to the efforts of the investor or the promoter but are arguably due to market forces. If that's the case, this prong isn't met, and there would be no investment contract. Thus, for example, if the value of my beach condo increases primarily because of low supply or high demand, as opposed to anything the developer does, then there is no investment contract.

C. Stock

"Stock" appears on the list of enumerated securities in the statutory definition of security. Does that mean that an instrument labeled "stock" is always a security for purposes of the federal securities laws? Usually, but not always.

The label is important, but not dispositive. Instead, the test turns on whether the stock has the characteristics typically associated with stock. These characteristics are:

- Can receive dividends
- Is freely transferrable
- Can be pledged
- Has voting rights proportionate to number of shares owned

- Can appreciate in value.

See United Housing Foundation, Inc. v. Forman, 421 U.S. 837 (1975).

The common stock that's issued by for-profit corporations has these characteristics. That means that the stock issued by public companies, such as Apple, Inc., is a security for purposes of the federal securities laws. And so is the stock that's issued by non-public companies, such as a small family-owned company.

More interesting questions pop up when an instrument is labeled "stock" but wasn't issued by a for-profit corporation. For example, in *United Housing Foundation, Inc. v. Forman*, a developer sold "stock" in an affordable housing co-op. You might remember from your 1L Property class that when a purchaser buys a co-op apartment, the purchaser doesn't buy the actual apartment. Instead, the purchaser buys shares of stock in the housing cooperative that owns the building. In *Forman*, the housing cooperative couldn't pay dividends. Moreover, the stock wasn't freely transferable. Instead, the purchasers could only transfer the stock back to the co-op at the price the purchaser initially paid for the stock. Finally, voting rights were apportioned as one vote per apartment, as opposed to one vote per share. Because the housing co-op stock lacked the characteristics typically associated with "stock," the Supreme Court held it wasn't "stock" for purposes of the federal securities laws.

But remember that if an instrument labeled stock isn't "stock" within the meaning of the federal securities laws, it could still be a security. How? If it's an investment contract! That's actually the second part of the *Forman* case, where the Supreme Court held that the *Howey* test wasn't met. The first prong wasn't met because the purchasers bought the stock so that they would have a place to live—*i.e.*, the purchasers had a consumption motivation, not investment motivation.

D. Interests in Partnerships and Limited Liability Companies

Most of us would probably consider interests in partnerships and limited liability companies to be securities. The problem, though, is that they aren't on the laundry list of enumerated securities contained in the statutory definition of "security." Therefore, the only way they can be regulated under the federal securities laws is if they are investment contracts—which gives us another opportunity to review the *Howey* test.

1. Partnership Interests

General Partnership Interests. Let's get right to it: the general rule is that general partnership interests are not investment contracts. That's because the fourth prong of the *Howey* test—which requires that a third party is primarily responsible for any profits—is usually not met. One of the defining characteristics of a general partnership is that each partner has equal rights in the management of the partnership's business. In other words, general partners are not passive investors; they control the partnership. This means that the success of the investment *is* primarily due to each partner's efforts.

However, like all general rules, there are exceptions. If the general partners of a general partnership don't actually control the general partnership, then the partnership interests might constitute investment contracts. This can happen in three ways:

1. The partnership agreement reduced the management power of the general partners so significantly that they no longer control the general partnership; they are more like limited partners in a limited partnership;

2. The general partners are so inexperienced and unknowledgeable in "business affairs" that they aren't capable of exercising control over the general partnership; or

3. The general partners are so dependent on some unique entrepreneurial or managerial ability of the promoter or manager that they can't replace the manager or otherwise exercise meaningful control over the partnership.

These are commonly referred to as the *Williamson* factors, after the name of the case that first identified them. *See* Williamson v. Tucker, 645 F.2d 404 (5th Cir. 1981).

The first *Williamson* factor applies when the partnership agreement changes the statutory default rule so that the general partners become passive investors. This might happen, for example, if the partnership agreement provides that the partnership will be managed by a managing partner elected by the general partners. To decide if this *Williamson* factor applies, you would have to review the terms of the partnership agreement and determine how much power was taken away from the general partners. It has to be a lot—enough to turn the general partners into *de facto* limited partners.

The second *Williamson* factor applies when a general partner theoretically has control over the general partnership, but the partner isn't sophisticated enough to exercise it. In effect, then, the general partner is passive—meaning the fourth prong of *Howey* is met. The issue that courts struggle with—and that you may have to struggle with—is determining what *Williamson* meant by a lack of sophistication in "business affairs." Does "business affairs" mean general business knowledge? Or does it mean knowledge about the general partnership's specific business? Or both? For example, what if a Chief Financial Officer of a public company decided to invest for the first time in the opening of a hip new restaurant? She entered into a general partnership agreement. As a CFO, she would be extremely sophisticated about business, but, as a first-time investor in a restaurant, she would be extremely unsophisticated about the restaurant business. Most courts focus on lack of sophistication about the partnership's business.

Finally, the third *Williamson* factor applies when the general partnership includes a "rock star" manager who is seen as the reason the partnership will be successful. To get back to my restaurant example, what if an internationally renowned restaurateur is the promoter of the general partnership? Legally, this restaurateur is a general partner, no different than any other general partner. Legally, she only has one vote. But practically, she runs the show. The only reason this venture will be successful is her efforts. The other general partners are completely dependent on her skills, making them passive investors. Note that the bar for the *Williamson* factor is quite high: the person skills must be "unique."

Limited Partnership Interests. The general rule is that limited partnership interests are investment contracts. That's because, by statute, limited partners have very limited voting rights, making them passive investors. Therefore, the fourth prong of the *Howey* test—which requires that a third party is primarily responsible for any profits—is usually met.

However, the general rule won't apply if the limited partnership agreement gives the limited partners voting rights so that they're no longer passive. In that case, the limited liability interests won't be investment contracts.

2. *Limited Liability Company Interests*

Whether interests in limited liability companies are investment contracts depends on the type of LLC: member-managed or manager-managed. Once again, the fourth prong of *Howey* is typically the key issue.

Member-Managed LLC Interests. Member-managed LLC interests are typically not investment contracts. That's because in a member-managed LLC, each member has equal rights in the management of the LLC. Just like general partners in a general partnership, members of a member-managed LLC are not passive investors. Therefore, the fourth prong of *Howey* isn't met—unless the *Williamson* factors apply.

Manager-Managed LLC Interests. On the other hand, membership interests in manager-managed LLCs are typically investment contracts. The members a rely on the manager; the members are passive. Therefore, the fourth prong of *Howey* is met.

E. Promissory Notes

Notes are on the list of enumerated securities, but they are not necessarily securities for purposes of the federal securities laws. Think about the promissory note that's signed when you get a mortgage. Or when you finance your car. Or when you take out a student loan. Congress didn't intend to regulate these consumer or commercial transactions through the federal securities laws. Therefore, courts have had to determine which notes are securities and which aren't.

Over time, courts have put together a list of notes that aren't securities for purposes of the federal securities laws. For example, courts decided that the following notes aren't securities:

- Notes secured by mortgage
- Notes delivered in consumer financing
- Notes evidencing a bank's loan to a customer

But what if a note isn't on this list? You should apply the *Reves* family resemblance test to see if the note resembles a note on the list of "not-securities" or to see if you can add a new note to the list of "not-securities." *See* Reves v. Ernst & Young, 494 U.S. 56 (1990).

Under the *Reves* family resemblance test, we start with the rebuttable presumption that all instruments labeled "notes" are securities. To rebut the presumption, you need to consider the following factors:

- The motivations of lender and the borrower
- The plan of distribution
- The reasonable expectations of the investing public
- The existence of risk-reducing factors

Let's talk more about each of these factors.

1. *Motivations of Lender and Borrower*

If the lender's motivation is primarily to receive the interest payments from the note, then the note is more likely to be a security. On the other hand, if the lender's motivation is primarily to sell a consumer good or to advance a consumer purpose, then the note is less likely to be a security.

If the borrower's motivation is to raise money for the "general use" of a business or to finance "substantial investments," then the note is more likely to be a security. On the other hand, if the borrower's motivation is to purchase a consumer good or to correct the borrower's cash-flow problems, then the note is less likely to be a security.

2. *Plan of Distribution*

If the borrower's plan of distributing the notes will likely lead to trading in the notes, then the note is more likely to be a security. Trading may occur if, for example, the notes are offered to and/or held by a large number of people. That means that notes issued to a small number of people are less likely to be securities.

3. *Expectations of the Investing Public*

If the investing public reasonably expects the note to be regulated by the federal securities laws, then it's more likely to be a security.

4. *Existence of Risk Reducing Factors*

If the risks of the note are reduced, then the note is less likely to be a security. The risk of repayment could be reduced by specific provisions in the note itself. For example, the note could be secured with collateral or guaranteed by a third party. Or the risk of investment could be reduced because the note is already regulated by another law or regulatory authority.

Finally, we need to discuss the specific issue of short-term notes—which are defined as notes with a maturity date of less than nine months. Depending on the statute, these short-term notes may not be securities. Specifically, the '34 Act carves out from the definition of security any note "which has a maturity at the time of issuance of not exceeding nine months." *See* Securities Exchange Act of 1934 § 2(a)(1). Thus, for example, a note due in six months is never a security for purposes of the '34 Act; you don't even have to apply the *Reves* test. However, the '33 Act doesn't carve out short-term notes from the definition of security. *See* Securities Act of 1933 § 2(1). So, for example, a note due in six months would be a security for purposes of the '33 Act—unless the *Reves* test rebuts the presumption.

The *Reves* test can be hard to apply because it's highly fact dependent. In addition, it's a holistic test. It's not clear how many of the *Reves* factors are needed to rebut the presumption of security. Moreover, it's not clear whether any one (or more) of the four *Reves* factors is more important than the others. Nonetheless, let's give it a try.

Let's assume that a company borrows money through a bridge loan. A bridge loan provides temporary funding to a company until it's able to obtain a more permanent financing solution, such as a stock offering. Typically, these notes have a one-year maturity date. However, if the stock offering closes before the note's maturity date, the note becomes due upon that closing and will be paid out of the offering proceeds. The interest rate of a note issued in a bridge loan is generally higher than other notes. Is the note a security?

We start by noting that notes are an enumerated security. Therefore, the note is presumed to be a security.

Then we apply the *Reves* family resemblance test. The lender's motivation is clear: it is lending the money to obtain a high interest rate, which makes it more likely that the note is a security. The borrower's motivation is also clear: to correct a short-term cash flow problem by financing the company until it receives the proceeds of a stock offering. This motivation makes it less likely that the note is a security. So in this case, the *Reves* test cuts both ways. Not particularly helpful.

Typically, only a small number of wealthy and sophisticated investors are approached to lend money in a bridge financing. Therefore, no trading market in this note will likely develop. This factor makes it less likely that this note is a security.

We would need more facts to determine the reasonableness of the lender's beliefs. The note and related documents might explicitly disclaim that they are regulated by the federal securities laws, making it less likely that the note is a security. Even without a disclaimer, a sophisticated and experienced lender probably understands that a bridge loan isn't the kind of note that's typically regulated by the federal securities laws.

Finally, there are two risk reducing factors in bridge loans. First, the loans are secured. So long as the value of the collateral exceeds the principal amount of the note, the risk of the note has been reduced. And second, the note will be repaid first out of the permanent financing, reducing the risk of repayment. These factors make it less likely that the note issued in a bridge financing is a security.

Remember that the *Reves* test is holistic: look at all the facts together. Here, although some facts indicate that the note is a security, there's a good argument that there the presumption should be rebutted. The borrower's motivation, the plan of distribution, and the presence of risk reducing factors all point to this note not being a security. This conclusion is buttressed by a recognition that Congress probably didn't intend to regulate relatively low-risk notes that were issued to a small group of lenders.

F. Quick Recap

There are different tests to determine if different instruments are securities. That means that the first thing you need to do is determine the correct test to use.

Start with the name of the instrument or the name of venture. Does it appear on the list of enumerated securities? If no, then apply the *Howey* test to determine if this is an investment contract. All four prongs must be met to create an investment contract. If it's not an investment contract, it's not a security.

If the name does appear on the list of enumerated securities, the appropriate test is determined by the name of the instrument.

If the instrument is labeled "stock," then apply the *Forman* test. This requires you to see if the instrument has the characteristics typically found in stock. If the instrument has these characteristics, then it's stock for purposes of the federal securities laws. If not, it's not stock.

If the instrument is labeled "note," then apply the *Reves* test, which is a rebuttable presumption that notes are securities under the federal securities laws. This presumption can be rebutted by analyzing the four factors set forth in *Reves*.

If you determine that stock isn't "stock" or that a note isn't a "note" for purposes of the federal securities laws, remember that the instruments can still be securities if they meet the *Howey* test.

CHAPTER 3

Public Offerings: The Registration Process

A. Introduction

A public offering occurs when a company—referred to as the "issuer"—offers securities to anyone and everyone—*i.e.*, to the public. Remember that public offerings by sketchy promoters were the driving force behind the '33 Act. Following the Crash of 1929, Congress determined that investors needed to be provided with extensive information before they should be allowed to purchase securities in a public offering. Therefore, today, when an issuer makes a public offering, it's required to prepare and file with the SEC a lengthy disclosure document called a "Registration Statement." In general, the issuer can't *offer* securities to the public before it files the Registration Statement with the SEC. Moreover, the issuer can't *sell* securities in a public offering until the SEC declares the Registration Statement to be "effective." *See* Securities Act of 1933 § 5.

It can be a little challenging to understand how public offerings are regulated, primarily because the rules vary depending on the type of company that's making the public offering. We know that the SEC tries to balance the competing goals of investor protection and capital facilitation, and we see this on full blast in the rules regulating public offerings. In short, the SEC recognized that not all companies selling securities to the public should be regulated in the same way. Companies going public require the most regulation. These companies haven't filed information with the SEC before, meaning that the public doesn't know much about these companies. To ensure informed decision making, the public needs to be given comprehensive information about the company and the offering.

On the other hand, companies that are already public are already required to file periodic reports—the annual report on Form 10-K and quarterly reports on Form 10-Q—and proxy statements with the SEC. The investing public doesn't need as much information to make informed decisions about whether to purchase securities in a public offering made by an already public company. And, finally, certain public companies are so well-known to investors and market professionals that maybe the SEC doesn't need to regulate them at all.

We'll get into more of the specifics below, but the SEC has created four categories of issuers:

- ***Non-reporting issuers***: companies that aren't required to file periodic reports with the SEC under the '34 Act; *i.e.*, private companies
- ***Unseasoned issuers***: public companies that are required to file periodic reports with the SEC, but aren't large or established enough to be treated as seasoned issuers or well-known seasoned issuers
- ***Seasoned issuers***:
    - public companies that have been public for at least one year and have a public float of at least $75 million; or

  - public companies that have been public for at least one year with a public float of less than $75 million, so long as they sell no more than one-third of the company's public float in any 12-month period

- ***Well-Known Seasoned Issuers (WKSIs)***: public companies that have been public for at least one year and either (1) have a public float of at least $700 million; or (2) have registered more than $1 billion of debt to the public in the last three years

We'll start with the regulation of public offerings by non-reporting issuers—the initial public offering (IPO)—and then continue to public offerings by the other kinds of issuers.

B. Public Offerings by Non-Reporting Issuers: The Initial Public Offering

1. Non-Reporting Issuers

A non-reporting issuer is a company that isn't required to file periodic reports, such as the annual report on Form 10-K, with the SEC. These kinds of companies are also referred to as "private" companies because they haven't sold securities to the public before.

2. The Decision to Go Public

An initial public offering occurs when a non-reporting issuer offers securities to the public for the first time. You've probably seen videos of someone ringing the bell on the floor of the New York Stock Exchange. Why does this person look so happy? It's often because this person is the CEO of a company that's just gone public.

Companies go public for various reasons. The first and most obvious reason is to raise money. Sometimes a LOT of money. For example, in 2024, Reddit went public and raised close to $750 million in its IPO. And there are other benefits. For example, when a company goes public, its stock will trade on a national securities exchange, such as the New York Stock Exchange (NYSE) or Nasdaq. This provides its shareholders with a cheap and easy way to sell their stock, which makes them very happy. An IPO also provides early investors with a way to exit the company. In addition, because many individuals prefer to work for public companies, going public may attract better employees. Finally, going public generates publicity, highlighting the company's operations and increasing its profile with investors, customers, and suppliers.

But there are significant costs to going public. First are the direct costs, such as accounting fees, legal expenses, filing fees, and printing costs. These costs are especially high in an IPO because non-reporting companies are for the first time required to have audited financial statements. And the costs keep coming because once a company goes public, it becomes subject to the ongoing disclosure costs of being a reporting company. It will have to file periodic reports with the SEC and prepare proxy statements for the annual shareholder meeting. Moreover, going public means that the company can't keep its results confidential anymore; its competitors will know things about the company they never knew before. It also requires an investment of time by senior management, distracting them from running the business. Once public, management will also have to worry about disappointing analysts. Every quarter, management will have to worry about its stock price. In addition, if the price of the company's stock falls unexpectedly, the company will likely face securities fraud class actions. So going public isn't an easy decision to make.

3. The Underwriting Process

Once the non-reporting issuer has decided to go public, the first thing it needs to do is find someone who actually knows how to sell securities to the public. This will be the "underwriter." The names of some of the biggest underwriters might be familiar to you: investment banks such as Goldman Sachs, J.P. Morgan, and Morgan Stanley.

The underwriter will provide a variety of services to the issuer, including determining the price that the securities will be offered to the public. IPOs are "fixed price" offerings; *i.e.*, the stock will be sold at a pre-determined price, such as $10 per share. Since no trading market existed for the issuer's securities before the IPO, it's not easy to come up with the appropriate price. The underwriter will have to carefully gauge interest in the issuer and the overall health of the markets to come up with the public offering price. If the price is set too high, there may not be buyers for the stock. On the other hand, if the price is set too low, the issuer didn't raise as much money as it could've. This is referred to as "leaving money on the table."

The underwriter's most important responsibility, however, is to find purchasers for the issuer's securities. They will do this in one of two ways: a "best efforts" underwriting or a "firm commitment" underwriting.

A best efforts underwriting is just like it sounds: the underwriter promises to use its best efforts to find purchasers for the issuer's offering. In return, the underwriter will receive a flat fee for its work. There are three types of best efforts underwritings: straight, all or none, and mini-max.

In a straight best efforts offering, the issuer must sell whatever stock was purchased, even if less the total amount of the offer. For example, assume that an issuer hopes to raise $10 million by offering 1 million shares of stock at $10 per share. If the underwriter managed to find purchasers for only 800,000 shares, the issuer will be required to sell the 800,000 shares and will receive $8 million from the sale (less the underwriter's fee).

Some issuers might be happy with raising $8 million, but, for other issuers, this $2 million shortfall might be a big problem. For example, if an issuer determined that it needed to raise at least $10 million to continue its business, raising anything less than $10 million won't help. In this kind of case, the underwriter will typically condition the best efforts underwriting on selling all 1 million shares of stock. This is called an "all or none" best efforts underwriting. If the underwriter found purchasers for only 800,000 shares, no stock would be sold. Any collected sales proceeds would be returned to the purchasers.

Finally, there is the "mini-max" best efforts underwriting. In this kind of case, the underwriter will condition the best efforts offering on finding purchasers for a specific amount of stock. For example, if the issuer would be okay with raising anywhere between $7.5 million and $10 million, the underwriter would condition the best efforts offering on selling at least 750,000 shares of stock. If the underwriter found purchasers for 800,000 shares, the condition would be met, and 800,000 shares would be sold. On the other hand, if the underwriter found purchasers for only 700,000 shares, no stock would be sold, and any collected sales proceeds would be returned to the purchasers.

Most issuers prefer firm commitment underwritings. In a firm commitment, the underwriter actually purchases the securities from the issuer at a discount and then re-sells the securities to the public at the public offering price. The underwriter's fee is the difference between the discounted purchase price and the public offering price, usually 7% in IPOs. For example, assume once again that the issuer is offering 1 million shares of stock at $10 per share.

In a firm commitment offering, the underwriter is obligated to purchase all 1 million shares for $9.30 per share and then resell the shares to the public at the public offering price of $10 per share.

As you can see, in a firm commitment underwriting, as opposed to the best efforts underwriting, the underwriter bears the risk of finding purchasers for the stock. If the underwriter in a firm commitment can't find purchasers, the underwriter gets stuck with owning the stock. This is pretty much of a disaster for the underwriter. Not only does it tie up the underwriter's capital, which could limit its ability to underwrite other offerings, it's a big hit to the underwriter's reputation. Therefore, the underwriter takes several steps to make sure it doesn't get stuck with a "sticky" offering.

Many of these protections are found in the "underwriting agreement" between the issuer and the underwriter, such as the "market out" provision. Similar to a *force majeure* clause, the market out clause allows the underwriter to walk away from the public offering if there have developments that would make it difficult for the underwriter to find purchasers for the securities.

However, the most effective way for the underwriter to reduce the risk is to find other underwriters that will share the risk. The underwriter hired by issuer becomes the "managing underwriter" of this "underwriting syndicate." The managing underwriter allots each member of the syndicate a percentage of the firm commitment offering to purchase and then re-sell.

4. The Registration Statement

While the managing underwriter is working with the underwriting syndicate to line up purchasers for the company's securities, the issuer's lawyers are working on the Registration Statement. The SEC has created several "forms" of registration statement. The form that must be used by a company going public is the Registration Statement on Form S-1.

The Form S-1 contains comprehensive information about the issuer and about the offering. For example, the issuer must provide the following types of information about the company:

- The company's business
- The company's board of directors
- The company's senior management
- The company's major stockholders
- Executive compensation
- Several years of financial statements, including balance sheets and income statements, that have been audited by an independent accounting firm
- Management's discussion and analysis of its financial condition (the MD&A)
- Information about the effectiveness of the company's internal controls
- Copies of the company's organizational documents and important contracts.

The issuer must also provide the following types of information about the offering:

- The price of the securities
- A description of the securities being sold
- A description of the type of underwriting
- The offering's risk factors
- How the proceeds of the offering will be used.

Sometimes lawyers use the term "Prospectus" interchangeably with the term "Registration Statement." While these terms are related, they refer to two different disclosure documents. The Registration Statement is the document filed with the SEC, while the Prospectus is the document that's distributed to investors. The Prospectus contains most, but not all, of the information that's contained in the Registration Statement. In fact, if you look at a Form S-1, you'll see that it's organized into two parts: "Part I: Information Required in Prospectus" and "Part II: Information Not Required in Prospectus." We'll talk more about the Prospectus in Chapter 4.

As you can probably imagine, Registration Statements are very long documents. In an IPO, the Form S-1 is typically several hundred pages long—and that's without including the exhibits! That's a lot of disclosure.

5. Emerging Growth Companies

If you can believe it, the amount of disclosure in IPOs used to be even more extensive. But it's been reduced for "Emerging Growth Companies." Being an EGC opens the door to several benefits, including streamlined disclosure requirements, both in the Form S-1 and in subsequent '34 Act filings. For example, the Form S-1 calls for non-EGCs to provide audited financial statements for three years. However, EGCs are only required to provide audited financial statements for two years. That's quite a cost savings.

What does it take to be classified an EGC? It's a defined term. Under Rule 405 of the '33 Act, a company qualifies as an EGC if it had total annual gross revenues of less than $1.235 billion during the last year and hadn't sold any common stock to the public in the past. Issuers can keep the EGC classification for no more than five years. Nowadays, most issuers of IPOs qualify as EGCs.

6. *Integrated Disclosure*

The specific information that issuers must disclose in the Registration Statement is set forth in what are called "Items." For example, take a look at the Form S-1 (which can be found in your statutory supplement or at the SEC's website). Notice that there are 16 different disclosure Items.

Now take a look at "Item 11(a)" of the Form S-1. This item requires the issuer to describe its business. But Item 11(a) doesn't actually tell us what kind of information about the issuer's business must be disclosed. Instead, Item 11(a) tells us to provide the information required by Item 101 of Regulation S-K. In other words, the issuer has to follow the bouncing ball from Item 11(a) of the Form S-1 to Item 101 of Regulation S-K to find out what information about the company's business must be disclosed in the Form S-1.

At first glance, this seems silly. Why require the extra step? The answer is that this creates what the SEC calls an "integrated disclosure" system. Regulation S-K sets forth most of the SEC's disclosure requirements for non-financial information. All SEC's filings—both '33 Act filings and '34 Act filings—refer to Regulation S-K. For example, if a form requires disclosure of information about the company's business, the form will refer to Item 101 of Regulation S-K. This assures us that the description of the company's business will be exactly the same, whether it's disclosed in a Registration Statement on Form S-1 under the '33 Act or an Annual Report on Form 10-K under the '34 Act. Integrated disclosure cuts down on differing and duplicative disclosure, which reduces the disclosure costs to companies. Thus, it furthers the SEC's goal of facilitating capital formation.

7. Filing the Registration Statement with the SEC: The Waiting Period

Once the issuer and the underwriter are happy with the Registration Statement, the issuer will file the Form S-1 with the SEC. Nowadays, for most issuers going public, this is a two-step process. First, the issuer *submits* a draft Registration Statement to the SEC for confidential review. After receiving the SEC's comments, the issuer might decide it's not ready to go public after all and may pull its public offering. In this case, the Registration Statement remains confidential, meaning that any sensitive financial and non-financial information that's in the draft Registration Statement will remain secret.

Most issuers, however, will decide to continue with their public offerings after submitting draft Registration Statements. In this case, the issuer will then *file* its Registration Statement with the SEC. This filing—and any previous draft Registration Statements—will now be publicly available. The SEC will also provide comments on the filed Registration Statement. In its comments, the SEC often asks the company to make additional disclosures or to clarify certain disclosures in the Registration Statement. In response, the company usually amends its Form S-1 to reflect the SEC's comments. This back-and-forth will go on several times, leading to numerous amendments to the Registration Statement.

8. Effectiveness

After several months, if all goes well, the SEC will finally sign off on the Registration S-1. Upon the issuer's request, the SEC will issue an order, called a "Notice of Effectiveness," which provides the date and time the Registration Statement will become effective. When the Registration Statement is effective, the issuer can finally sell its securities.

C. Public Offerings by Companies That Are Already Public Companies

1. Overview

Companies that are already public often decide to raise additional capital by selling more of their securities to the public. Because investors and market professionals already have information about these already-public companies, these public offerings are treated differently than an IPO. The SEC gives preferential treatment to some of these public companies, such as:

- Form S-3: Some reporting issuers are allowed to use a different form of registration statement—the Form S-3—that is more streamlined than the Form S-1
- Shelf-Registration: some reporting issuers are allowed to use shelf registration—as discussed in more detail below—to raise money
- Automatic Effectiveness: Some reporting issuers won't have to wait for SEC review to start selling securities; instead, the registration statement becomes automatically effective upon filing with the SEC

All of these preferences are designed to make it cheaper and faster for these companies to raise capital.

2. *The Registration Statement on Form S-3*

The Registration Statement on Form S-3 allows the issuer to satisfy many of the '33 Act's disclosure requirements about the company by incorporating by reference into the Form S-3 some of the company's filings made under the '34 Act, such as the periodic reports on Forms 10-K, 10-Q, and 8-K, and the company's proxy statement. "Incorporation by reference" is a method of making a second document become part of a main document simply by using the "incorporation by reference" language and referencing the second document. This means that the Form S-3 doesn't include much information about the issuer. The idea is that there's no need to repeat it in the actual Form S-3 because investors are already aware of it. Note that this is possible because of the integrated disclosure system discussed above.

So what information is disclosed in the Form S-3? Information that hasn't already been disclosed by the public company in its '34 Act reports. In general, that means information about the offering, such as the price of the securities, a description of the securities being sold, a description of the type of underwriting, the offering's risk factors, and how the proceeds of the offering will be used.

Not all offerings by already-public companies can be made on Form S-3. The offering must be *eligible* for Form S-3. The eligibility criteria are set forth in General Instruction I to Form S-3.

First, under General Instruction I.A, only **certain issuers** are eligible. The issuer must:

- Be a U.S. corporation
- Be a '34 Act reporting company
- Have timely filed reports with the SEC for at least 12 months
- Have filed one Annual Report on Form 10-K with the SEC
- Be in good financial health.

Second, only *certain offerings* can be registered on Form S-3. General Instruction I.B sets forth a list of six offerings that qualify, but we'll focus on the offerings used by public companies to sell common stock for cash. They are described in Instruction I.B.1 and Instruction I.B.6.

Offerings by Qualified Issuers with a $75 Million Public Float. Under General Instruction I.B.1, a qualified issuer may use Form S-3 to sell common stock for cash if the issuer has a public float of at least $75 million. "Public float" is defined as the aggregate market value of the common stock that isn't owned by insiders of the company. So, for example, assume that a company had 10 million shares outstanding, trading at $10 per share on the NYSE. The company's float would be $100 million. But if 4 million of those shares were held by company insiders, its public float would be only $60 million. This company, therefore, would not be able to rely on Instruction I.B.1 to use Form S-3 to register its offering.

Why the $75 million public float requirement? The SEC often uses public float as an approximate measure of how widely a stock is followed by analysts and other market professionals. The more widely followed, the more likely it is that the investing public is informed about the company, reducing the need for mandatory disclosure. The SEC has determined that companies with a public float of $75 million is the magic number.

Limited Offerings by Qualified Issuers with Less than a $75 Million Public Float. What about public companies that don't have a $75 public float? Under General Instruction I.B.6, these qualified issuers can use Form S-3 to sell common stock for cash, but the amount of stock they can sell is subject to what's referred to as the "one-third cap." Specifically, in any 12-month period, a qualified issuer can only sell up to one-third of the aggregate market value of the company's public float. In addition, the issuer's common stock must trade on a national securities exchange, as opposed to trading over-the-counter or on the "pink sheets."

As an example, assume a qualified issuer has a public float of $60 million. Because its public float is less than $75 million, it could not rely on Instruction I.B.1 to use Form S-3. However, if the company wanted to sell $15 million of common stock, it could rely on Instruction I.B.6 to use Form S-3. That's because the $15 million offering would be under the one-third cap. For you math-phobes out there, remember that one-third of $60 million is $20 million.

Public companies that can use Form S-3 to register offerings of securities for cash under General Instruction I.B.1 or I.B.6 are called "seasoned issuers." Public companies that can't use Form S-3 to register offerings for cash under General Instruction I.B.1 or I.B.6 are called "unseasoned issuers."

3. Shelf Registration

The general rule is that when a company sells securities to the public, it must sell the entire offering immediately. An issuer can't register an offering now, get the SEC to issue an order of effectiveness, and then wait to sell the securities in the future. Put another way, the company can't register an offering, put the securities on the shelf, and then take the securities off the shelf when the issue decides to offer them to the public—hence the term "shelf registration." The concern with shelf registration is that the information in the Registration Statement might be outdated or incorrect when the company finally decides to issue the securities to the public.

Like most general rules, there are exceptions. And the exceptions are found in Rule 415 of the '33 Act—the shelf registration rule. Shelf registrations can only be made pursuant to Rule 415. Rule 415 contains exceptions for 13 different types of shelf offerings. Most of them are there for pragmatic reasons. For example, think of a company that has issued convertible debt. This company needs to be able to issue the common stock underlying the debt as soon as the holder converts the debt. Without shelf registration, the issuer would have to go through SEC review, which would take months. But that wouldn't work for the holder, who wants the stock now! Therefore, the issuer needs to be able to have shares of common stock ready to be issued that can be taken off the shelf and immediately issued when the convertible debt is converted. The SEC recognized this need and provides for this type of shelf registration in Rule 415(a)(1)(iv).

Note that only one of the 13 exemptions set forth in Rule 415 authorizes a company to use a shelf registration to raise money, and that's the exception we'll focus on. It's found in Rule 415(a)(1)(x).

This kind of shelf registration is extremely advantageous to issuers. Think of a public company that knows it wants to issue additional shares of stock but believes that now is not the best time to sell them. Under Rule 415(a)(1)(x), this company can register the offering now and then wait until the market is more attractive. When market conditions improve, the company can move quickly and sell stock immediately to the public because the registration statement has already been declared effective.

Every public company wants to be able to use this kind of shelf registration, but Rule 415(a)(1)(x) only allows offerings that are qualified to be registered on Form S-3 to be registered for the shelf. That means that only seasoned issuers can raise capital through a shelf registration as follows:

- Offerings by a qualified issuer—the company has been public for at least a year—with a public float of at least $75 million
- Offerings by a qualified issuer—the company has been public for at least a year—with a public float of less than $75 million, so long as the issuer is selling no more than one-third of its public float; this is often called a "baby shelf" registration

Rule 415 imposes a few additional conditions on this kind of shelf registration. First, the Form S-3 is only effective for three years, although the issuer can file a new registration statement to extend effectiveness. Second, the issuer must provide an "undertaking"—essentially a promise—to update its Form S-3 to reflect "fundamental changes" to the company that occurred after the Form S-3 was declared effective.

The Form S-3 used in a shelf registration won't be very lengthy. Most of the company-specific information will be incorporated by reference from the issuer's '34 Act reports. Moreover, there won't be much offering-specific information because the company doesn't have that information yet. When a company files a shelf registration with the SEC, it won't know what securities it will be offering, what the sales price will be, who the underwriter will be, or what the proceeds will be used for. This information won't be available until the company decides to sell. Therefore, issuers are allowed to provide very general information about the offering. *See* Securities Act of 1933 Rule 430B. The Prospectus used in a shelf registration under Rule 415(a)(1)(x) is called a "Base Prospectus."

In a shelf-registration, the Form S-3 is filed with the SEC and will go through the SEC comment process. When the SEC declares the Registration Statement effective, the issuer, rather than immediately selling its securities to the public, will wait until market conditions are optimal. When the issuer does decide to sell, it will do a "take down" of the securities. At this point, information about the offering will now be known, and the Base Prospectus will be supplemented to reflect the final terms of the security and the offering. This document is referred to as a "Prospectus Supplement" or the "Pro-Supp." The issuer will choose the underwriter, which will proceed with the offering.

4. *Automatic Effectiveness*

Finally, for some very lucky public companies, their Registration Statements on Form S-3 will become effective automatically upon filing with the SEC. This means that there will be no review by the SEC before the issuer can sell its securities—which saves the issuer significant time and money. This preference is limited to "Well-known Seasoned Issuers," commonly referred to as "WKSIs"—which is pronounced Wick-sees.

In creating the WKSI category, the SEC intended to identify the largest and most active issuers in U.S. capital markets. Approximately 30% of listed companies are WKSIs, and they account for 95% of U.S. equity market capitalization and 96% of the total debt raised in registered offerings. The idea is that these companies are so well known by investors and market professionals that the concern for investor protection is significantly reduced.

What are the legal requirements to qualify as a WKSI? Rule 405 defines a WKSI as a public company that has been public for at least one year and either (1) has a public float of at least $700 million; or (2) has issued more than $1 billion of non-convertible debt to the public in the last three years. In addition, if an issuer qualifies as a WKSI on debt grounds, as opposed to public float grounds, and wants to take issue common stock, it must have a public float of at least $75 million.

To obtain automatic effectiveness, all the WKSI has to do is check the appropriate box on the front cover of the Registration Statement on Form S-3.

5. *Summary of What Public Companies Get What Preferences*

Type of Issuer	Can Use Form S-3 to Raise Capital	Can Raise Capital Using Shelf-Registration	Registration Statement Is Automatically Effective upon Filing with SEC
Non-Reporting Issuer	No	No	No
Unseasoned Issuer	No	No	No
Seasoned Issuer	Yes	Yes	No
WKSI	Yes	Yes	Yes

D. Alternatives to the Traditional IPO

Recently, some companies have gone public without using the traditional IPO process, such as through a SPAC transaction or a direct listing.

1. *SPACs*

A SPAC transaction is a two-step process. First, the promoters form a special purpose acquisition company (SPAC). A SPAC is a corporation created for the express purpose of acquiring an existing unspecified non-public company sometime in the next 18-24 months. If the SPAC doesn't find a target within the timeframe, it must return the IPO proceeds to the investors.

Because investors in the SPAC don't know what company the SPAC will acquire, a SPAC is sometimes referred to as a "blank check" company. The promoters of the SPAC raise money for the acquisition by going public through a traditional registered IPO. When the registration statement becomes effective, the SPAC's stock will trade on a national securities exchange.

The second step occurs when the SPAC identifies the non-public company it wants to acquire. It will enter into a friendly merger agreement with the non-public company, which is commonly referred to as the "de-SPAC" transaction. In the de-SPAC transaction, the SPAC and the non-public company will merge. The merged companies will then change the name of the traded stock to the name of the formerly non-public operating company. Voila! The formerly non-public company is now a public company.

Why use a SPAC to go public? First, the registration process for the SPAC proceeds very quickly because there's not much information to disclose about the SPAC in the registration statement. In addition, because the non-public company doesn't go through the registration process at all, it avoids the time and expense of going public. Finally, for the non-public company, the de-SPAC transaction may be viewed as a more certain approach to going public than a traditional IPO, especially in times of crisis.

On the other hand, SPACs have been criticized as being bad for the public investors. The SPAC registration statement doesn't contain much information because there's not information to be given about a blank check company. And the SPAC's Form S-1 generally receives less scrutiny by the SEC. Moreover, SPACs are riskier than traditional IPOs because the SPAC's public investors are rolling the dice on the company the SPAC decides to acquire. Moreover, the SPAC structure can be seen as inherently unfair to the public investors. The sponsors make money even when the public investors don't. Moreover, the pressure to find a non-public company target within 18-24 months could cause the SPAC to choose unfavorable companies to merge with just to avoid having to pay back the investors.

SPACs reached their highest popularity in 2021—during the COVID epidemic. Since then, very few companies have chosen to go public in a SPAC transaction.

2. *Direct Listings*

Historically, a direct listing occurs when a non-public company registers the previously-issued securities of existing shareholders for sale to the public through the NYSE or Nasdaq.

Because the company isn't registering an offering of newly-issued stock, it won't be raising any capital. Since IPOs are generally used to raise money, that would seem to be a big drawback to the direct listing. However, if the company doesn't need to raise capital and is just looking to create a trading market for its securities, the direct listing might be a good option. The company will get its stock listed on an exchange and do that without diluting their existing shareholders. There are several other benefits. First, in a direct listing the securities aren't sold through a fixed price offering; they're sold at whatever price is being offered on the securities exchange. Therefore, there's no danger of leaving money on the table. Moreover, because a direct listing doesn't involve an underwriter, the issuer saves a lot of money in underwriting fees and expenses.

E. Quick Recap

The public offering process is highly regulated to ensure that investors can make informed decisions about whether or not to buy securities in the offering. The required information is contained in a Registration Statement. An issuer can't offer securities to the public before it files a Registration Statement with the SEC, and the issuer can't sell securities in a public offering until the SEC declares the Registration Statement to be "effective."

The SEC recognizes that not all public offerings are the same. Non-reporting issuers and unseasoned issuers subject to more regulation than seasoned issuers and WKSIs. As a reminder, non-reporting issuers and unseasoned issuers are required to use the Registration Statement on Form S-1, which requires issuers to disclose the most information about the company and the offering. Seasoned issuers and WKSIs are permitted to use a shorter form of registration statement—the Form S-3—to register their offerings. Moreover, seasoned issuers and WKSIs can take advantage of shelf registration to raise capital, which allows them to register securities now and sell them in the future. Finally, WKSIs are in the best position of all because their shelf registrations become automatically effective upon filing. Thus, WKSIs enjoy almost instantaneous access to the capital markets. My strong advice is to make sure you know the difference between the four types of issuers.

CHAPTER 4

Gun Jumping: Regulating Communications During the Registration Process

A. Introduction

The heart of the '33 Act is Section 5. That's the provision that prohibits companies from selling securities to the public until the SEC declares the Registration Statement to be effective. But in addition to requiring issuers to prepare a Registration Statement, Section 5 limits what issuers can do and say during the registration process. Securities lawyers refer to these restrictions as "gun jumping" rules. Why gun jumping? Think of a competitive runner or swimmer who starts the race before the gun goes off. They've jumped the gun. The same can be said for a company who offers or sells securities before it's allowed to do so under Section 5.

If you read Section 5 closely, you'll see that it creates three different time periods: the pre-filing period, the waiting period, and the post-effective period. Each period has different restrictions.

Issuer files Registration Statement with the SEC

SEC declares Registration Statement Effective

Pre-filing Period	**Waiting Period**	**Post-Effective Period**
Can't offer securities for sale Can't sell securities	**Can** offer securities for sale under limited circumstances Can't sell securities	**Can** offer securities for sale with some restrictions **Can** sell securities
Section 5(c) Section 5(a)	Section 5(b)(1) Section 5(a)	Section 5(b)(1) Section 5(b)(2)

Section 5 sets forth the general gun jumping limitations, but the SEC has adopted a lot of rules that loosen the restrictions found in Section 5, making it easier and cheaper for issuers to raise capital. Several of these rules are available only to seasoned issuers and/or WKSIs.

To be honest, the gun jumping rules can get pretty complicated. Some professors dig deep and devote multiple classes to gun jumping. Other law professors give gun jumping a lighter touch. The following discussion tries to keep it short and happy; I'd describe it as medium coverage.

B. Pre-Filing Period

Gun jumping starts with the "pre-filing period." It begins when the company chooses its managing underwriter and continues until the company files its Registration Statement with the SEC. During the pre-filing period, Section 5 prohibits issuers from offering or selling securities. In addition, as explained below, due to the broad definition of "offer," issuers have to be very careful about making any type of communication to the public during the pre-filing period or risk having the communication found to be an impermissible offer. In fact, for this reason, securities lawyers often refer to the pre-filing period as the "quiet period."

1. Section 5(c) and the Definition of "Offer"

The prohibition on offers is clear. Section 5(c) states that "[i]t shall be unlawful for any person, directly or indirectly, . . . to offer to sell or offer to buy . . . any security, unless a registration statement has been filed as to such security . . ." Thus, the regulatory focus during the pre-filing period is on the "offer."

Why did Congress prohibit offers during the pre-filing period? Investor protection. The idea is that an issuer shouldn't be allowed to offer securities to the public unless the public has access to a disclosure document containing all the information needed to make an informed decision about whether to purchase securities in the offering. This information won't be available until the Registration Statement is filed with the SEC.

That means it's important to understand the definition of offer. Section 2(a)(3) of the '33 Act includes a definition, but it's not helpful. So it's been left to the courts and the SEC to define it. An offer certainly includes an express offer to sell or buy securities. For example, if an issuer takes out an ad in *The Wall Street Journal* offering 10 million shares of stock for sale, that's an offer.

But the definition also includes implied offers. According to the SEC, an implied offer includes communications by an issuer that "condition the market" or "arouse public interest" in the offering. The concern is that these kinds of communications are the first step in marketing the offering to potential investors. These communications might cause potential investors to get worked up about investing in the offering—but the potential investors wouldn't have the full story about the offering. For example, they wouldn't have received all the relevant information about the offering, including the offering's risks.

The SEC's broad definition of offer creates difficult problems for companies in the pre-filing period. Companies—especially public companies—regularly communicate with their customers, suppliers, shareholders, and the press. How do we know whether these communications are impermissible offers?

For example, assume that ABC, Inc. decided to go public. On the same day that ABC chose its managing underwriter, it also approved a new advertising campaign for its products, which included commercials to appear on television (including the Super Bowl). Previously, ABC's advertising was limited to social media. In addition, for the first time, the new advertising campaign used a very popular and recognizable celebrity as a spokesperson. The advertising stressed the quality of ABC's products and stated that "nationwide, consumers prefer ABC's products over its competitor by a margin of more than three to one." Is this just advertising? Or is it also an offer to sell securities?

The issuer would certainly argue that this was advertising. The SEC, however, would likely argue that this was an offer. Which is it? And how do we figure it out?

Basically, it turns on the issuer's motivation. Was ABC really trying to advertise its products to consumers? Or was its true intent to start marketing the offering to investors? Over time, through a series of releases, the SEC has provided guidance about the factors that could cause the SEC to infer that the issuer's motive was to start its offering.

Generally, it's okay for issuers to continue the communications they've done in the past. Therefore, an issuer is permitted to:

- Advertise its products and services, if consistent with past practice
- Disseminate factual information, if consistent with past practice

- Respond to unsolicited inquiries about the company's business, if consistent with past practice
- Hold regularly-scheduled shareholder meetings, if consistent with past practice
- Speak at trade shows and industry meetings, if consistent with past practice

As you can see, the key is whether the issuer's behavior is "consistent with past practice."

On the other hand, if the issuer makes changes to the content or form of the above communications, the SEC may become suspicious that the company is actually beginning its offering. This is especially so if the timing of the change seems to suggest that it was made in response to the upcoming public offering.

In addition, the SEC has indicated that issuers in the pre-filing period shouldn't:

- Make predictions regarding the company's future increased earnings, market share, growth, or stock price
- Issue opinions about the company's valuation
- Identify the name of the underwriter

This brings us back to ABC's advertising campaign discussed above. Is it an offer? On the one hand, ABC is advertising its products, which the SEC has said is okay. On the other hand, ABC departed substantially from its past practice: it changed the content of its advertising and the type of advertising from social media to television. And it did this around the time it decided to go public. Therefore, the SEC would likely conclude that ABC was motivated to make these changes to arouse public interest in the company's upcoming public offering, not to advertise its products. In other words, ABC made an impermissible offer during the pre-filing period.

If this is found to be an offer, the issuer won't be happy. That's because the SEC will probably delay the company's public offering, reasoning that investors needed a "cooling off period" after the company's impermissible offer. In addition, it exposes the company to liability under the '33 Act, which we'll talk more about in Chapter 7.

2. *Criticisms of the Gun Jumping Rules During the Pre-Filing Period*

The pre-filing period's gun jumping rules have their detractors. One obvious criticism is the difficulty in applying the SEC's "arousing public interest" and "conditioning the market" definition of offer. It can be a trap for the unwary, creating obstacles for issuers to raise capital in public offerings. Lawyers have been complaining about this to the SEC for years.

There's another problem, too. The ban of offers during the pre-filing period makes it difficult for non-reporting issuers to figure out whether there is enough investor interest to justify going public—what securities lawyers refer to as "testing the waters." That's because asking potential investors whether they might be interested in buying securities in a particular offering is an offer, which isn't permitted by the gun jumping rules. This means that non-reporting issuers might go through all the expense of preparing for a public offering, only to find out that investors aren't interested. If they had been aware of the lack of interest, the issuers wouldn't have pursued the IPO.

More generally, critics argue that the ban on offers during the pre-filing period doesn't make sense. As we know, the purpose of the ban is to stop potential investors from making uninformed decisions to buy securities in public offerings. At first glance, that seems to make sense. But what's the real harm to investors? After all, during the pre-filing period, the potential investors—no matter how excited they became because of the offer—can't actually buy the securities. Sales can't be made until the post-effective period. That would be weeks, if not months, in the future. By that time, the Registration Statement would be filed, and the potential investors would have access to all the information they would need to make an informed decision. And, presumably, if the offer had led to the potential investor becoming excited about the IPO, the passage of time would have allowed the excitement to cool down.

3. Permissible Activities During the Pre-Filing Period

Eventually, the SEC responded to these criticisms by adopting several safe harbors, exemptions, or exclusions from Section 5(c). They are:

- Rule 169: Limited Safe Harbor for Communications of Regularly Released Factual Business Information
- Rule 168: Limited Safe Harbor for Communications of Regularly Released Factual Business Information and Forward Looking Information
- Rule 163A: 30 Day Bright Line Exclusion
- Rule 163: Exemption from Section 5(c) for Certain Communications by WKSIs
- Rule 135: Notice of Proposed Registered Offering
- Rule 163B: "Testing the Waters"

Rule 169: Safe Harbor for Communications of Regularly Released Factual Business Information. Rule 169 is supposed to help attorneys determine whether an issuer's communication of business information constitutes an offer. Under Rule 169, "the regular release or dissemination by or on behalf of an issuer of communications containing factual business information shall be deemed not to constitute an offer to sell or offer for sale of a security . . . if the conditions of this section are satisfied." Under the rule, "factual business information" includes advertising about the company's products and services.

Rule 169 is modeled on the SEC guidance discussed above, so the conditions won't be a surprise to you. They are:

- The issuer must have previously disseminated factual business information in the ordinary course of its business;
- The timing, manner, and form of dissemination is consistent in material respects with similar past disseminations; and
- The information is targeted to the issuer's customers and suppliers, not investors of the issuer's securities.

Note that Rule 168 doesn't protect information about the upcoming securities offering.

Rule 169 can be used by all issuers, including non-reporting issuers in their IPOs.

Rule 168: Limited Safe Harbor for Communications of Regularly Released Factual Business Information and Forward Looking Information. At first glance, Rule 168 looks very similar to Rule 169, but there are two significant differences. First, Rule 168 provides a safe harbor for both factual business information as well as forward looking information, such as predictions regarding the company's future increased earnings, market share, growth, or stock price. Second, Rule 168 permits information to be targeted to investors of the issuer's securities.

Rule 168 can only be used by seasoned issuers and WKSIs.

Rule 163A: 30 Day Bright Line Exclusion. Rule 163A provides that any communication made by issuer more than 30 days before the date the issuer files its Registration Statement with the SEC won't be an offer—so long as the communication doesn't reference the securities offering. The idea behind this exclusion is that the passage of thirty days should cool the enthusiasm of the potential investors.

Rule 163A can be used by all issuers, including non-reporting issuers in their IPOs.

Rule 163: Exemption from Section 5(c) for Certain Communications by WKSIs. Rule 163 is another example of a preference given to WKSIs under the federal securities laws. According to Rule 163, all communications by WKSIs—no matter the content, the form, or the intended audience—are exempt from the gun jumping rules during the pre-filing period. This means that WKSIs can make offers during the pre-filing period.

The only conditions apply to written offers. Written offers have to include a legend recommending that the investor should read the prospectus before investing, and they must be filed with the SEC.

Only WKSIs can use Rule 163.

Rule 135: Notice of Proposed Registered Offering. You might be wondering how companies can announce an upcoming public offering during the pre-filing period without violating the gun jumping rules. The safest way to do this is through Rule 135, which states that a "notice" of a proposed offering won't constitute an offer so long as the notice includes a required legend and includes no more than the limited information permitted by the rule. This permitted information consists of basic information about the offering, such as the name of the issuer, the title, amount, and basic terms of the securities that are being offered, the anticipated date of the offering, and a brief statement of the manner and purpose of the offering—without naming the underwriters. If any additional information is included in the notice, Rule 135 isn't available.

All issuers can use Rule 135.

Rule 163B: "Testing the Waters." The SEC responded to the complaint that the gun jumping rules prohibited issuers from "testing the waters" by adopting Rule 163B. Under this rule, issuers are expressly allowed to communicate with certain investors to determine if they're interested in a future securities offering. However, issuers can contact only "Qualified Institutional Buyers" or "Institutional Accredited investors." As we'll see in Chapter 5, Qualified Institutional Buyers—commonly referred to as "QIBs" and pronounced "Kwibs"—are the largest and the most sophisticated category of institutional investor. QIBs include asset management companies, banks, hedge funds, insurance companies, and mutual funds that invest at least $100 million. Institutional Accredited Investors are institutional investors—*i.e.*, not individuals—that don't qualify as QIBs but meet Regulation D's definition of "accredited investor." We'll talk more about Regulation D and accredited investors in Chapter 5.

All issuers can use Rule 163B.

C. Waiting Period

Once the issuer files its Registration Statement with the SEC, the waiting period begins. It continues until the Registration Statement is declared effective by the SEC. During this period, the issuer is still prohibited from selling its securities. But the issuer can finally begin to offer its securities for sale—although there are certain limitations on how the offers can be made. The waiting period is when the issuer's main selling efforts take place.

1. Section 5(b)(1) and the Definition of Prospectus

Section 5(b)(1) prohibits issuers from making an offer though a prospectus, unless the prospectus meets the requirement of Section 10 of the '33 Act. That means that the regulatory focus during the waiting period is on the "prospectus."

What is a prospectus? It's defined in Section 2(a)(10), but it largely boils down to a written offer.[1] With advances in technology, the definition of "writing" has expanded to include all "graphic communications," which include communications made via email, websites, audio and videotapes, and blast voicemails. *See* Securities Act of 1933 Rule 405.

All written offers are considered prospectuses, but only certain prospectuses can be used during the waiting period. They must comply with Section 10. To comply with Section 10, the prospectus must include the information listed in Section 10(a). In general, that means that the prospectus must include most of the information that's in a Registration Statement. As we know from the previous chapter, that's an awful lot of information. A Section 10(a) prospectus is referred to as a "final prospectus."

Thus, when the '33 Act was enacted, Congress envisioned that during the waiting period, written offers could only be made through a formal document that contained most of the same information included in the Registration Statement. Once again, it's all about investor protection: ensuring that investors are fully informed about the offering.

As an example, assume that ABC, Inc. filed a Registration Statement with the SEC. A broker then sent an email to her best customers to let them know about the offering and urged them to invest. The email is a written offer. Therefore, it's a prospectus.

---

[1] The definition also includes an offer made by radio or television. *See* Securities Act of 1933 § 5(b)(1).

However, the email obviously doesn't contain the same information as a Registration Statement. Therefore, the email didn't meet the requirements of Section 10. Section 5 has been violated.

2. Permissible Activities During the Waiting Period

At first glance, Section 5(b)(1) appears to be very restrictive. However, SEC rules have liberalized the gun jumping rules during the waiting period. Nowadays, issuers communicate with potential investors in a variety of ways during the waiting period, including:

- Oral Offers
- Rule 430: Preliminary Prospectus
- Rule 164: Free Writing Prospectus
- Rule 163B: "Testing the Waters"
- Rule 134: Identifying Statement
- Rule 134(d): Indications of Interest
- Rule 433: Road Shows

Oral Offers. Oral offers are permitted because they aren't prospectuses. Remember that a prospectus is a *written* offer. That means that brokers can call their clients during the waiting period and offer to sell them securities without violating the gun jumping rules.

Preliminary Prospectus. The preliminary prospectus is the most common way that offerings are marketed during the waiting period. A preliminary prospectus contains most of the information that appears in the Registration Statement—other than the price of the securities and information that's derived from the price. The preliminary prospectus has a specific legend on the front cover that warns investors that the prospectus isn't final. This legend is printed in red ink—which is why preliminary prospectuses are sometimes referred to as "red herrings."

This means that preliminary prospectuses can be emailed and distributed to potential investors during the waiting period. They can also be posted on social media and websites during the waiting period.

Preliminary prospectuses don't run afoul of the gun jumping rules because Rule 430 says that they don't. Remember that Section 5(b)(1) prohibits issuers from making an offer though a prospectus, unless the prospectus meets the requirement of Section 10 of the '33 Act. Rule 430 specifically states that a preliminary prospectus "shall be deemed to meet the requirements of section 10 of the Act for the purpose of section 5(b)(1)." That means that preliminary prospectuses automatically meet the waiting period's gun jumping rules.

Rule 430 comes from a grant of power that's expressly set forth in Section 10(b). Section 10(b) permits the SEC to authorize prospectuses to be used during the waiting period, even if they don't include all of the information that's in a Registration Statement. These are referred to Section 10(b) prospectuses. The preliminary prospectus is the prime example of a Section 10(b) prospectus.

Free Writing Prospectus. The issuer can also make written offers during the waiting period as long as they're accompanied or preceded by a preliminary prospectus. *See* Securities Act of 1933 Rule 164. This type of written offer is called a "free writing prospectus." The FWP rules reflect the SEC's recognition that investors aren't harmed by written offers during the waiting period—as long as they've been provided with a copy of the preliminary prospectus. After all, the preliminary prospectus presumably contains everything the investor needs to know to make an informed investment decision.

The FWP rules are a little complex, so stay with me! First, let's make sure we understand what a FWP is. According to Rule 405, a FWP is any written offer—*i.e.*, a prospectus—other than a Section 10(a) or Section 10(b) prospectus. To get an idea of what this means, some examples of FWPs are emails or blast voicemails encouraging potential investors to buy securities in the offering, PowerPoint presentations disseminated to potential investors, positive media articles about the offering, and term sheets or summaries of the terms of the offering that have been posted on websites.

Without the FWP rules, these written communications would violate the gun jumping rules because they are prospectuses that don't satisfy Section 10. However, under Rule 164, a FWP that meets the conditions of Rule 433 will be deemed to be a Section 10(b) prospectus. This means that Section 5(b)(1) will automatically be met.

Rule 433 sets forth several conditions, including a legend and filing requirement, to using the rule, but the most important condition is that the preliminary prospectus must "accompany or precede" the FWP. Non-reporting issuers and unseasoned issuers must actually deliver a copy of their preliminary prospectus to investors to meet this requirement. On the other hand, seasoned issuers and WKSIs don't have to deliver the preliminary prospectus; it's enough that they have filed a copy of their preliminary prospectus with the SEC. In other words, the SEC is equating "access" to the preliminary prospectus with "delivery" of the preliminary prospectus. Obviously, access is cheaper. However, after balancing investor protection and facilitating capital formation, the SEC determined that only seasoned issues and WKSIs would get this this cost-savings preference.

To sum up, let's revisit the above example of the broker who sent an email to her best clients, encouraging them to purchase stock in ABC's upcoming offering. This time, the broker included a hyperlink to ABC's preliminary prospectus in the email. Did this email violate the gun jumping rules? Note that there are two prospectuses in this example: the email is a prospectus, and the preliminary prospectus is a second prospectus. We know that the preliminary prospectus is okay under Rule 430. But what about the email? Is it okay under the FWP rules?

I'd suggest using the following approach:

- First, is the email a FWP? Yes. The email is a written offer, and it's not a Section 10(a) or Section 10(b) prospectus.
- Second, did a preliminary prospectus accompany or precede the FWP? Yes; by linking to the preliminary prospectus in the email, the broker ensured that the preliminary prospectus accompanied the FWP.
- Third, is actual delivery required? Actual delivery was required because ABC was a non-reporting company. Therefore, assuming that Rule 433's legend and filing conditions were met, the email didn't violate the gun jumping rules.

Testing the Waters. Just like the pre-filing period, during the waiting period, issuers are allowed to test the waters with QIBs and Institutional Accredited Investors. Rule 163B expressly states that these communications will be exempt from Section 5(b)(1).

Identifying Statements. Upon filing its Registration Statement with the SEC, issuers usually issue a press release announcing that they've launched their public offering. Rule 134 permits this communication if it includes only the limited content listed in the rule. The limited content includes basic information about the company and the offering (including a description of the securities, the number of securities being offered, the estimated offering price, the use of proceeds, the names of the underwriters, and the date of the offering). Rule 134 also requires the communication to include a legend notifying potential investors that the securities can't be sold yet and informing them that they can obtain a copy of the preliminary prospectus. These communications are referred to as "identifying statements."

Indications of Interest. Issuers are also allowed to send limited written information to potential investors so that they can indicate whether they're interested in purchasing securities in the offering. If these conditions are met, Rule 134(d) provides that these "indications of interest" won't be considered prospectuses. Most importantly, the indication of interest can only include the information that's permitted in the identifying statement and it must be accompanied or preceded by a preliminary prospectus.

Road Shows. For issuers, the "road show" is a crucial part of the registration process. During the waiting period, members of the issuer's senior management team, together with the underwriters, typically meet with large institutional investors to pitch the public offering to them. In the old days, top executives would get on a plane and fly around the country (and sometimes the world) to persuade these mutual funds and asset managers to become long-term investor in their company. Hence, the term "road show." These days issuers can also make their presentations virtually.

During the road show, management typically makes a PowerPoint presentation to the institutional investors and answers their questions. Usually, a short video is shown and copies of the PPT are distributed to the attendees. How are these communications permissible during the waiting period?

The oral presentation and statements made during the Q&A are clearly permissible because they're oral offers. As discussed above, oral offers aren't prospectuses, so they don't violate Section 5(b)(1). The video and copies of the PowerPoint presentation are in writing, so they would seem to be subject to the gun jumping rules.

The SEC has taken the position, however, that written communications that are provided at a live road show are deemed to be part of the road show. In other words, as long as the written communications are collected at the end of the presentation, they're considered to be part of the road show's oral communications, and therefore not prospectuses. *See* Securities Act of 1933 Rule 433(d)(8).

One other thing about road shows . . . they're often recorded and broadcast to other investors, such as individual, or retail, investors, sometime after the live road show. This changes the gun jumping analysis. Because the recorded road show isn't a live event, it's no longer considered to be an oral offer. Instead, the recording will be treated as a free writing prospectus, and the issuer must satisfy the FWP conditions of Rule 433, as described above.

D. Post-Effective Period

Once the SEC has declared the Registration Statement to be effective, we enter the post-effective period, which lasts for at least 25 days following the date of effectiveness. Finally, the issuer can sell its securities!

At this point, you're probably thinking that the gun jumping rules are over. But you would be wrong. Our old friend Section 5(b)(1)—which regulates the use of the prospectus during the waiting period—also applies during the post-effective period. In addition, a new subsection of Section 5—Section 5(b)(2)—also applies to the post-effective period. Therefore, there are three gun jumping issues that arise during the post-effective period:

- Prospectuses
- Confirmations of sales
- Delivery of securities

1. Prospectuses

Since Section 5(b)(1) applies during the post-effective period, we have to make sure that any prospectuses used after the Registration Statement becomes effective meet the requirements of Section 10. There are three ways that prospectuses can be used during the post-effective period.

First, a final prospectus, also called a Section 10(a) prospectus, can be used. The final prospectus includes the price of the stock, as well as all information derived from the price. Note that a preliminary prospectus can't be used during the post-effective period; it only be used during the waiting period.

Second, if the written offer isn't a final prospectus, it can still be used if it's accompanied or preceded by the final prospectus. If this sounds familiar, you're right. It sounds an awful lot like the FWP rules discussed above. However, this is different. Here, it's permitted by Section 2(a)(10)(a), which states that written offers made during the post-effective period won't constitute prospectuses if the investor was provided with a copy of the final prospectus. This is sometimes referred to as "statutory free writing" because it is permitted by the '33 Act itself. It was permitted even before the FWP rules were adopted by the SEC. In fact, the purpose of the FWP rules was to extend the statutory free writing permitted during the post-effective period to the waiting period.

Finally, the written offer can be made pursuant to the FWP rules discussed above. Note that Rule 164 and Rule 433 apply to communications made after the Registration Statement has been filed, which includes both the waiting period and the post-effective period. Why would an issuer use the FWP rules, rather than statutory free writing? The FWP rules are more attractive to seasoned issuers and WKSIs because they're not required to deliver a copy of the final prospectus. For them, access to the final prospectus equals delivery. For non-reporting companies and unseasoned issuers, statutory free writing is usually the more attractive option.

2. *Confirmations of Sales*

When a securities transaction is made, the federal securities laws require brokers to send a written confirmation of sale to their customers. That makes a lot of sense. What may not make a lot of sense is that a confirmation of sale is a "prospectus" for purposes of Section 5. Surprise!

How can that be? The answer is that Section 2(a)(10) includes a second definition of prospectus: a written confirmation of sale. Thus, sending a confirmation of sale would appear to violate Section 5(b)(1) because the confirmation of sale doesn't contain the information that's found in a Registration Statement. In the past, the way to do it would be through statutory free writing—*i.e.*, sending a copy of the final prospectus. Nowadays, it's done through Rule 172(a).

Rule 172(a) states that if the issuer has filed a copy of the final prospectus with the SEC, the confirmation of sale is exempt from Section 5(b)(1). This is another example of the SEC adopting the "access equals delivery" approach to information.

3. *Delivery of Securities*

When a sale is made during the post-effective period, a stock certificate representing the purchased stock might be sent to the purchaser. Section 5(b)(2) makes it unlawful to send a security through the mail unless the security is accompanied or preceded by a final prospectus. However, the SEC essentially eliminated this obligation in Rule 172(b). Under Rule 172(b), if the issuer has filed a copy of the final prospectus with the SEC, the requirements of Section 5(b)(2) are deemed to be satisfied. Once again, "access equals delivery" eases the burden on issuers, which facilitates capital formation.

Note that nowadays, most purchasers don't even receive a stock certificate. Instead, their stock is held in their broker's name—*i.e.*, "street name"—and the brokers keep track of stock ownership. So, in this case, Section 5(b)(2) wouldn't be triggered.

E. Quick Recap

If you get a gun jumping question on your exam, the first thing you should do is identify the relevant period: pre-filing, waiting, or post-effective. Once you do this, you can determine what the regulatory focus is. Tell your professor what part of Section 5 is relevant.

In addition, identify whether the company selling securities is a non-reporting issuer, an unseasoned issuer, a seasoned issuer, or a WKSI. You'll need to know this to determine whether certain SEC rules are available.

If the question involves the pre-filing period, you should be looking for impermissible offers. Remember that the definition of offer includes corporate communications if they "arouse public interest" or "condition the market." It helps to think like the SEC and be suspicious of the issuer's motivations in making the communication. Then look to see if any of the following SEC rules provide any help:

- Rule 169: Limited Safe Harbor for Communications of Regularly Released Factual Business Information
- Rule 168: Limited Safe Harbor for Communications of Regularly Released Factual Business Information and Forward Looking Information
- Rule 163A: 30 Day Bright Line Exclusion

- Rule 163: Exemption from Section 5(c) for Certain Communications by WKSIs
- Rule 135: Notice of Proposed Registered Offering
- Rule 163B: "Testing the Waters"

If the question involves the waiting period, you should be looking for prospectuses—written offers. Oral offers, including live in person road shows, aren't prospectuses. During the waiting period, prospectuses can be used only if they meet the requirements of Section 10. Then look to see if any of the following SEC rules provide any help:

- Rule 430: Preliminary Prospectus
- Rule 164: Free Writing Prospectus
- Rule 164B: Testing the Waters
- Rule 134: Identifying Statement
- Rule 134: Indications of Interest
- Rule 433: Road Shows

Note that the big legal issue here is the use of the FWP, so make sure you understand those rules.

Finally, if the question involves the post-effective period, you should once again be looking for prospectuses. Remember that a confirmation of sale is also a prospectus. Unless the issuer is using a final Section 10(a) prospectus, the issuer will have to rely on one of the following provisions:

- Section 2(a)(10)(a): Statutory Free Writing
- Rule 164 and Rules 433: Free Writing Prospectus
- Rule 172: Use of Prospectus in Post-Effective Period

CHAPTER 5

Unregistered Offerings Made Through Exemptions

A. Introduction

As we saw in Chapter 3 and Chapter 4, it's not easy to make a public offering. It's expensive, and the registration process takes a long time to complete. Wouldn't it be great for your clients to be able to raise money without having to prepare a Registration Statement and without having to wait for the SEC to issue the notice of effectiveness? They can—as long as the offering is made pursuant to an exemption.

By "exemption," we mean an exemption from Section 5. Exemptions are found in Section 3 and Section 4 of the '33 Act. As we'll see, even more exemptions have been created by the SEC.

If an exemption is available, the issuer will be able to sell securities without registering the offering. That means that investors won't have the information they need to make an informed decision about whether to invest in the offering. Thus, exemptions seem to raise significant investor protection concerns. So . . . why do we have exemptions?

It boils down to a cost-benefit analysis. Sometimes, the benefits of registration are outweighed by its costs. In other words, exemptions reflect a balancing of the two policies underlying the '33 Act: protecting investors and facilitating capital formation.

Think of a start-up company that needs to raise $5 million to continue its operations. The securities will be sold to a handful of wealthy "angel" investors or venture capital firms. For this start-up company, the need to raise capital is especially acute, but the costs of registration will be high. And registration will delay the offering. Are the costs of registration justified for such a small offering? And one that involves only a handful of investors? And is registration really needed to protect the sophisticated purchasers in this offering who can presumably protect themselves by bargaining for any information they need? No, to all of these questions. So, not surprisingly, we'll see that offerings like this are usually exempt from registration.

Each exemption has different conditions. Sometimes, the conditions are imposed to make sure that investors can still make informed investment decisions, even though the offering isn't registered. Examples of this type of condition include limiting sales to sophisticated investors or requiring issuers to provide some kind of disclosure document to investors.

Other conditions are designed to make sure that investors won't suffer too much financial harm from investing in unregistered offerings, such as limiting sales to wealthy investors or limiting the dollar amount of securities that an investor can purchase in the offering.

Finally, some exemptions include conditions to reduce the number of investors that could be harmed by the unregistered offering. Examples of this type of condition include limiting the number of purchasers who can participate in the offering, prohibiting advertising of the offering, and restricting resales of securities purchased in the unregistered offering.

Often, an exemption has multiple conditions—reflecting the SEC's attempt to balance protecting investors and facilitating capital formation. Here's a list of the most common conditions that might attach to an exemption:

- Issuer Eligibility Requirements
- Limitations on Offering Amount
- Limitations on Number of Purchasers
- Limitations on Investment Amount
- Required Disclosure Document
- Investor Eligibility Requirements
- Limitations on the Manner of Offering
- Resale Restrictions
- SEC Filing Requirements
- Ongoing SEC Reporting Requirements

Most likely, your professor will expect you to be able to identify the exemptions that are available for a potential offering and, if more than one exemption is available, to determine which exemption would be the best exemption to use. I've found that the best way to do this is to put the information into charts so that it's easy to compare exemptions. And I've done this for you at the end of the chapter. You're welcome.

By the way, we won't be going through every possible exemption that's available under the '33 Act. To keep it short and happy, we'll be focusing on the most popular exemptions used by issuers to raise capital, which is what your professor is probably doing, too.

B. The Private Placement Exemption

Section 4(a)(2) sets forth the private placement exemption. It states that "transactions by an issuer not involving any public offering" are exempt from the registration requirements of Section 5. If the offering isn't public, it's private—hence, the name "private placement'' exemption. The '33 Act doesn't define what a "private placement" is. But the Supreme Court did. *See* SEC v. Ralston Purina Co., 346 U.S. 119 (1953).

In *Ralston Purina*, Ralston Purina sold stock to its "key" employees without registration. Ralston Purina argued that the private placement exemption was available because the offering wasn't open to the public; it was limited to certain employees. The SEC disagreed and sued the company for violating Section 5. The Supreme Court sided with the SEC, rejecting the argument that an offering limited to a specific group of people constitutes a "private" offering.

Instead, the Supreme Court adopted what is generally viewed as a two-pronged test, which asks:

- Do the offerees "need the protections of the ['33] Act"? [the "Information Prong"]
- Are the offerees "able to fend for themselves"? [the "Sophistication Prong"]

Ralston-Purina's two-part test imposes the following conditions:

Required Disclosure Document. The Information Prong of the *Ralston Purina* test requires that offerees must be provided with information similar to the information that's found in a Registration

Statement. This prong can be met by providing offerees with actual disclosure in the form of a Private Placement Memorandum or Offering Circular.

Alternatively, the Information Prong can be satisfied by providing offerees with effective access to information. In other words, the issuer could offer to provide the offerees with any information they want to review or to answer any questions the offerees have.

When the issuer is relying on access to satisfy the Information Prong, it has to be *effective* access. Think about potential purchasers who are unsophisticated. How would offering them access to information protect them? They wouldn't even know what documents to ask for. Not surprisingly, the Information Prong wouldn't be met in this circumstance. Additionally, even if the offerees are sophisticated, access won't help if they don't have the power to obtain the requested information from the issuer. Offerees with this power include senior officers of the issuer, family members of the founders of the issuer, and angel investors or a venture capital firm. Presumably, if any of these offerees were to ask for information from the issuer, they would get it.

Investor Qualification Requirements. The second prong of the *Ralston Purina* test makes clear that offerees must be sophisticated.

Determining sophistication can be difficult. It's a factual determination, and it must be done for each offeree. In general, in analyzing whether an offer is sophisticated enough to invest in a private placement, you should address the offeree's education level, occupation, and previous investment experience. In addition, although wealth isn't a proxy for sophistication, it's often considered a part of the sophistication analysis. We'll talk more about that when we discuss the definition of "accredited investor" below.

Limitations on the Manner of Offering. Issuers engaging in a private placement can't advertise or engage in general solicitation to find investors. This may be surprising to you because this limitation doesn't appear in Section 4(a)(2) and the Supreme Court didn't expressly impose it in *Ralston Purina*. However, it follows from the holding.

Remember that *Ralston Purina* is focused on protecting *offerees*, not purchasers. To use Section 4(a)(2), the issuer must show that the Information Prong and Sophistication Prong have been met for all offerees. But that would be impossible to do if the issuer, for example, advertised its offering in *The Wall Street Journal*. An advertisement is an offer to the entire world, and I think we can all agree that the entire world isn't sophisticated. That means the Sophistication Prong can't be met if the offering was advertised to the public. Thus, advertising and general solicitation is inconsistent with the private placement exemption. This makes it much harder, and much more expensive, to find investors—which is a big drawback to Section 4(a)(2).

Resale Restrictions. By resale restrictions, we mean that purchasers of securities aren't allowed to quickly resell the securities they purchased through an exemption. As we'll see, most exemptions have resale restrictions.

Section 4(a)(2) doesn't expressly set forth resale restrictions, and the Supreme Court didn't expressly impose them in *Ralston Purina*, but they're implicit. Without resale restrictions, issuers could easily evade an exemption's conditions by selling to an investor who meets the exemption's conditions knowing that the initial investor would immediately resell to investors who don't meet the exemption's conditions. That wouldn't make any sense.

Think of an issuer that sells securities to a qualified investor under Section 4(a)(2). The private placement exemption would be available. But if the qualified investor resold its securities the next day to an unsophisticated investor who didn't have effective access to information, that second investor would be harmed. Put another way, if the issuer couldn't use Section 4(a)(2) to sell directly to the second investor, then the issuer shouldn't be allowed to sell indirectly. The resale to an unqualified purchaser would invalidate the issuer's exemption. Lawyers often refer to this as a "blown" exemption.

To prevent a blown exemption, issuers take steps to prevent "downstream" resales. These resale restrictions typically include requiring all purchasers to agree not to resell the securities without the issuer's permission, placing legends on the stock certificates that state that the securities can't be freely resold, and directing the company's stock transfer agent not to transfer ownership of the stock without the issuer's permission. We'll talk a lot more about resales in Chapter 6.

C. Regulation D

1. Introduction

There's a lot to like about the private placement exemption, but there are definitely some drawbacks. Specifically, the uncertainty. For example, what does "sophisticated" mean? What information must be included in a PPM so that it counts as actual disclosure? How do we know whether an investor has effective access to information? To address these concerns, the SEC adopted Regulation D, which is widely used by issuers to raise capital without registration.

Regulation D contains three different exemptions: Rule 504, Rule 506(b) and Rule 506(c), which we'll go through in more detail below. But, before we get there, I want to drill down on two important concepts that run throughout Reg D: accredited investor status and the ban on advertising and general solicitation.

Accredited Investor Status. Reg D created a specific category of investor: the "accredited investor." *See* Securities Act of 1933 Rule 501(a). As we'll see, there are significant advantages associated with selling to accredited investors in a Reg D offering. So let's make sure we understand who qualifies to be an accredited investor. Accredited investors are:

- Market professionals and institutional investors, such as financial institutions, pension plans, mutual funds, investment advisers, broker-dealers, hedge funds, and venture capital firms
- Corporations with assets exceeding $5 million
- The directors and executive officers of the issuer
- Individuals with a net worth exceeding $1 million (not including the value of the investor's home)
- Individuals who have had an annual income of more than $200,000 (or more than $300,000 in joint income with the individual's spouse or spousal equivalent) for the last two years and who expect to have the same income in the current year
- Individuals who have certain professional certifications approved by the SEC, such as a license to sell to sell securities (Series 7 license), a license to provide investing and financial advice (Series 65 license), or a license to conduct private placements (Series 82 license)

Ban on Advertising and General Solicitation. Rule 502(c) imposes a ban on advertising and general solicitation on some offerings made pursuant to Reg D. Advertising includes offers published in newspapers, broadcast on radio or television, and posted on an issuer's website or social media accounts.

But what about offers made to a more targeted group of people? Are they permitted? It depends on whether these targeted offers constitute a "general solicitation." "General solicitation" isn't defined in Reg D, but, according to the SEC, a general solicitation has occurred if the issuer (or the person acting on behalf of the issuer) makes an offer without having a "pre-existing substantive relationship" with the offeree.

"Pre-existing" means a relationship that has already been established before the start of the offering. According to the SEC, "substantive" means that the issuer (or person acting on the issuer's behalf) "has sufficient information to evaluate, and does, in fact, evaluate, a prospective offeree's financial circumstances and sophistication, in determining his or her status as an accredited or sophisticated investor." *See* SEC Division of Corporation Finance Compliance and Disclosure Interpretations, Securities Act Rules, at Question 256.31.

For example, let's assume that I formed a company and I'm looking for additional investors. I think that my students might be interested in investing, so I make an offer to sell stock to the 40 students in my Securities Regulation class. Have I engaged in a general solicitation? Yes, I have. It's true that I have a pre-existing relationship with my students, but the relationship isn't substantive within the meaning of the '33 Act. Although I try to get to know my students, I don't know whether they're accredited or financially sophisticated.

On the other hand, what if I know that the offerees are accredited or sophisticated investors, but I don't have a pre-existing relationship with them? For example, what if I send emails to ten venture capital firms asking them to invest in my company? VCs are accredited and sophisticated investors, but I didn't have a relationship with them when I made my offer. That means my emails would constitute a general solicitation.

How can issuers find purchasers for their offering if they're not able to advertise or engage in general solicitation? There are two ways. First, the most popular way is to hire a financial firm that *does* have a pre-existing substantive relationship with qualified offerees. This financial firm would have a pool of potential investors that had been pre-qualified to invest in Reg D offerings. Because the financial firm would be working on behalf of the issuer, the issuer is able to rely on the financial firm's preexisting substantive relationship. Therefore, the issuer wouldn't be engaged in a general solicitation.

Second, the issuer could participate in a qualified "Demo Day." A "Demo Day" is an event, sponsored by community organizations, educational institutions, incubators, or investment groups, that provides an opportunity for the founders of a start-up to pitch their company to a group of potential investors. Often, these potential investors are so-called "angel investors"—very wealthy individual who qualify as accredited investors. If the sponsor pre-qualified the potential investors attending the Demo Day to ensure that they are accredited investors, this establishes the necessary pre-existing substantive relationship. Therefore, the Demo Day avoids becoming a general solicitation.

In addition, the SEC has adopted a safe harbor rule that expressly excludes certain "Demo Days" from the definition of "general solicitation." *See* Securities Act of 1933 Rule 148. Note that the safe harbor doesn't extend to Demo Days sponsored by venture capital firms or other groups whose primary purpose is to locate investors for companies.

As you can see, banning advertising and general solicitation makes it much more expensive to raise capital. The SEC argues that the ban is necessary to protect investors, but is it really? The ban reflects a commitment to protect offerees, not just purchasers. But why is it necessary to protect offerees who don't become purchasers? How are they harmed? The concern is that advertising and general solicitation will reach offerees who don't meet the requirements of the exemption. Presumably, because they wouldn't be eligible to invest, they would be screened out from purchasing securities. However, if an unqualified investor responds to an offer, an unscrupulous promoter might choose to take their money, anyway. Alternatively, an unqualified investor might lie to the promoters so that they would be able to get in on the offering. Once again, this would harm investors.

2. *Rule 504*

Remember that Reg D includes three different exemptions. The first is Rule 504. The justification underlying Rule 504 is commercial necessity: an exemption is needed to allow start-up companies to raise a small amount of capital. There's a lot to like about Rule 504. For example, any investor can invest, and the company doesn't have to put together a disclosure document. But there are several conditions:

Issuer Eligibility Requirements. Only non-reporting issuers can use Rule 504. *See* Securities Act of 1933 Rule 504(a). In addition, a non-reporting issuer that's a "bad actor" is disqualified from using this exemption. A "bad actor" is defined in Rule 506(d), but it essentially boils down to an issuer that doesn't deserve the exemption because the issuer, or one of its directors or officers or large shareholders, has been convicted of a securities-related crime.

Limitations on Offering Amount. An issuer can raise up to $10 million in any 12-month period pursuant to Rule 504. *See* Securities Act of 1933 Rule 504(b)(2). Obviously, this is Rule 504's most important condition.

Limitations on Manner of Offering. At first glance, Rule 504(b) appears to ban advertising and general solicitation, but then it sets forth three exceptions that are based on state securities laws, commonly referred to as "blue sky" laws. Advertising and general solicitation can be used in a Rule 504 offering if:

(i) The offering is made only in states that require the offering to be registered and require a disclosure document to be delivered to purchasers before sale; or

(ii) The offering is made in states that don't require the offering to be registered, but the offering has been registered in at least one state that does require registration and a disclosure document has been delivered to all purchasers before sale; or

(iii) The offering is only made through state exemptions that permit advertising and general solicitation so long as sales are made only to accredited investors.

These exceptions may seem overly complicated, but, once again, it has to do with the SEC trying to balance the goals of investor protection and facilitating capital formation. Rule 504 doesn't require a disclosure document—which seems to significantly undercut investor protection. But if investors receive a disclosure document required by state law, they will be protected. That's the idea behind exception (i) and exception (ii). Exception (iii) doesn't require a disclosure document, but it does require that all purchasers must be accredited investors. The SEC is less concerned about protecting accredited investors, who are more likely able to protect themselves.

Resale Restrictions. Yes, there are resale restrictions unless the offering was made pursuant to one of the three exceptions discussed above. *See* Securities Act of 1933 Rule 502(d). If these exceptions don't apply, the securities can't be freely resold.

SEC Filing Requirements. The issuer must inform the SEC that it has sold securities pursuant to Rule 504 by filing a short "Notice of Sale" on Form D with the SEC. *See* Rule 503.

3. Rule 506(b)

Rule 506(b) is a safe harbor for the private placement exemption, and it's probably the most popular of Reg D's exemptions. Rule 506(b)'s conditions are:

Limitations on Number of Purchasers. No more than 35 purchasers of securities can purchase securities in a Rule 506(b) offering. However, accredited investors don't count towards this number. Thus, put another way, issuers can use Rule 506(b) to sell to an unlimited number of accredited investors.

Required Disclosure Document. Yes, the issuer must furnish a disclosure document before any sales under Rule 506(b), unless all purchasers are accredited. *See* Securities Act of 1933 Rule 502(b). Put another way, the issuer won't have to furnish a disclosure document if it sells only to accredited investors.

If the issuer is a reporting company, this condition can be met by providing the company's annual report on Form 10-K and describing the terms of the offering. If the issuer isn't a reporting company, the company must provide basic information about the company and the offering that are consistent with Regulation A (described below). Audited financials are required if the offering exceeds $20 million.

Investor Eligibility Requirements. To use Rule 506(b), all purchasers must either be accredited or sophisticated. *See* Securities Act of 1933 Rule 506(b)(ii).

The definition of accredited investors is set forth above. "Sophisticated" means that the purchaser "has such knowledge and experience in financial and business matters that he is capable of evaluating the merits and risks of the prospective investment." *See* Securities Act of 1933 Rule 506(b)(ii). To make this determination, you'll be assessing factors such as the purchaser's occupation, education, and previous investment experience.

Limitations on Manner of Offering. Advertising and general solicitation are prohibited. *See* Securities Act of 1933 Rule 502(c). This is a big drawback to Rule 506(b).

By the way, in your Securities Regulation class, you might have come across Rule 241—a testing-the-waters provision for unregistered offerings—and thought that it might be used to find purchasers in Reg D offerings. However, asking potential investors if they would be interested in purchasing stock in an exempt offering would constitute a general solicitation if the issuer didn't have a pre-existing substantive relationship with them. That means that if a company used Rule 241 to test the waters, it probably wouldn't be able to use Rule 506(b). However, the SEC has stated that testing the waters communications under Rule 241 that are limited to qualified institutional buyers (QIBs) and institutional accredited investors would not constitute general solicitations. *See* Securities and Exchange Commission, Facilitating Capital Formation and Expanding Investment Opportunities by Improving Access to Capital in Private Markets, Rel. No. 33-10884 (Nov. 2, 2020).

Resale Restrictions. Securities acquired in a Rule 506(b) offering are considered restricted securities and can't be freely resold. *See* Securities Act of 1933 Rule 502(d).

SEC Filing Requirement. The issuer must inform the SEC that it has sold securities pursuant to Rule 504 by filing a Form D with the SEC. *See* Securities Act of 1933 Rule 503.

4. Rule 506(c)

If available, Rule 506(c) is probably the most attractive Reg D exemption because issuers can raise an unlimited amount of money, the company doesn't have to provide a disclosure document to purchasers, and advertising and general solicitation is permitted—a big advantage. However, to obtain these benefits, several conditions must be met:

Investor Eligibility Requirements. All purchasers must be accredited investors, and, not only that, they must be *verified* accredited investors. *See* Securities Act of 1933 Rule 506(c)(2). That means that the issuer must review the purchaser's tax filings, bank statements, brokerage statements, etc. to make sure that each purchaser is an accredited investor. The verification process is expensive and can be risky for the issuer.

Resale Restrictions. Securities acquired in a Rule 506(c) offering are considered restricted securities and can't be freely resold. *See* Securities Act of 1933 Rule 502(d).

SEC Filing Requirement. The issuer must inform the SEC that it has sold securities pursuant to Rule 504 by filing a Form D with the SEC. *See* Securities Act of 1933 Rule 503.

D. Intrastate Offering Exemptions

There are three different intrastate offering exemptions: Section 3(a)(11), Rule 147, and Rule 147A. There are several justifications for these exemptions. First, if an offering is occurring only in one state, the local investors don't need the protections of the federal securities laws. They'll already be knowledgeable about the issuer. Second, if an offering is purely local, state securities laws, rather than federal securities laws, should regulate it. This is more about federalism than investor protection.

1. Section 3(a)(11)

Section 3(a)(11) exempts purely local financings from Section 5. An example of a purely local financing would be a corporation incorporated and doing business in Pennsylvania offering and selling only to Pennsylvania residents. Section 3(a)(11)'s conditions attempt to ensure that the offering is, in fact, local:

Issuer Eligibility Requirements. The issuer must be incorporated and "doing business" in a single state. *See* Securities Act of 1933 § 3(a)(11). "Doing business" has been interpreted to mean a "significant" or "substantial" amount of business. To determine whether the issuer is doing business in the state, you should consider the location of its principal office, its assets, and its revenues, as well as where the proceeds of the offering will be used.

Investor Eligibility Requirements. The offerees and purchasers must be "residents" of a single state. This has been determined to mean domicile. You might remember the definition of domicile from your Civ Pro class. It requires both residency in that state and an intent to remain indefinitely in that state.

Limitations on Manner of Offering. Issuers can advertise and solicit purchasers, but any advertising and solicitation must be consistent with the intrastate nature of the offering. This limitation on the manner of the offering isn't mentioned in the statute, but it follows from the requirement that all *offerees* and purchasers must be resident in a single state.

For example, if a Pennsylvania corporation advertised its offering in *The Wall Street Journal* or through a social media post, that wouldn't be consistent with an intrastate offering because these forms of media are intended to reach a national audience, not primarily a Pennsylvania audience. On the other hand, if a Pennsylvania corporation advertised its offering in *The Philadelphia Inquirer*, that would be okay—because the newspaper is a

Pennsylvania periodical that primarily reaches Pennsylvania residents.

Resale Restrictions. Purchasers aren't permitted to resell their securities to residents of another state until the Section 3(a)(11) offering has "come to rest." We'll discuss this more in Chapter 6.

2. Rule 147

To address some of the uncertainties of Section 3(a)(11), the SEC adopted Rule 147 as a safe harbor for intrastate offerings. Not surprisingly, many of Rule 147's conditions are similar to Section 3(a)(11), but Rule 147 was intended to provide bright-line rules to help issuers plan their offerings. They include:

Issuer Eligibility Requirements. The issuer must be resident and doing business in a single state. Under Rule 147(c), an issuer is resident in a state if it is incorporated and has its principal place of business in a single state. Under Rule 147(c), an issuer will be deemed to be "doing business" in a state if one of the following requirements is met:

- At least 80% of the issuer's revenues are derived from that state;
- At least 80% of the issuer's assets are located in that state;
- At least 80% of the proceeds of the offering will be used in that state; or
- A majority of the issuer's employees are based in that state.

Investor Eligibility Requirements. Under Rule 147, the issuer doesn't have to worry about determining the domicile of investors.

Instead, Rule 147(d) requires that the offerees and purchasers must have their principal residence in that state.

Limitations on Manner of Offering. Just like Section 3(a)(11), issuers can advertise and solicit purchasers, but any advertising and solicitation must be consistent with the intrastate nature of the offering.

Resale Restrictions. Rule 147(e) imposes resale restrictions for six months following the offer. That means for the first six months, purchasers can only resell to other residents of the state. After the six month period, purchasers can sell to residents of other states.

3. *Rule 147A*

At first glance, Rule 147A might look a lot like Rule 147. But there are several important differences. First, corporations that are incorporated outside the state can use Rule 147A. In other words, an issuer incorporated in Delaware, with a principal place of business and doing business in Pennsylvania could use Rule 147A if the company sells only to Pennsylvania residents. In fact, this was one of the reasons that Rule 147A was adopted by the SEC. The SEC was aware that many companies, for the reasons you probably studied in your Business Organizations class, choose to incorporate in Delaware—even if they do business in only one state. But that means that these companies wouldn't be able use Section 3(a)(11) and Rule 147. To address this, the SEC promulgated Rule 147A.

Second, unlike Rule 147, which requires that both offerees and purchasers be resident of a single state, Rule 147A requires that only purchasers must be resident of a single state.

Finally, because offerees can be residents of other states, Rule 147A doesn't require that advertising must be consistent with the intrastate nature of the offering. National advertising and solicitation is permitted. This makes Rule 147A very attractive to issuers.

The conditions of Rule 147A are as follows:

Issuer Eligibility Requirements. The issuer must have its principal place of business and be doing business in a single state, but it is permitted to be incorporated in a different state.

Rule 147A uses the same definition of "doing business" as Rule 147. Thus, the issuer will be deemed to be "doing business" in a state if:

- At least 80% of the issuer's revenues are derived from that state;
- At least 80% of the issuer's assets are located in that state;
- At least 80% of the proceeds of the offering will be used in that state; or
- A majority of the issuer's employees are based in that state.

Investor Eligibility Requirements. Under Rule 147A, all purchasers must have their principal place of business in a single state.

Resale Restrictions. Rule 147A(e) imposes resale restrictions for six months following the offer. That means for the first six months, purchasers can only resell to other residents of the state. After the six month period, purchasers can sell to residents of other states.

E. Crowdfunding

The crowdfunding exemption permits start-up companies to use the Internet to raise capital from a large number of investors who each invest a small amount of money. The SEC wanted to give regular investors—not just accredited investors—the opportunity to invest in start-ups. Investor protection concerns are alleviated because the rule imposes strict limits on the amount investors can purchase. Moreover, crowdfunding is premised on the "wisdom of the crowd" theory of investing. A crowd of investors will communicate with each other, leading to more informed investors.

Crowdfunding is authorized by Section 4(a)(6) of the '33 Act, and the SEC then fleshed out the exemption through a series of rules in Regulation Crowdfunding. There are numerous conditions to the crowdfunding exemption:

Issuer Eligibility Requirements. The crowdfunding exemption can only be used by non-reporting companies.

Limitations on Offering Amount. Issuers can use the exemption to raise up to $5 million in any 12-month period.

Limitations on Investment Amount. Accredited investors can invest as much as they want, but non-accredited investors are limited in the amount of money they can invest in a crowdfunding offering based on the greater of their annual income or net worth. *See* Regulation Crowdfunding § 227.100(a)(2). Specifically:

> (i) If either the investor's annual income or net worth is less than $124,000: the greater of $2,500 or 5% of the greater of the investor's annual income or net worth
>
> (ii) If both the investor's annual income and net worth are equal to or more than $124,000: 10% of the greater of the investor's annual income or net worth, not to exceed $124,000

How does this work? Assume that Alice has a net worth is $150,000 and an annual income of $80,000. What's the most she can invest in a crowdfunding offering? Since she's not an accredited investor, she's subject to limitations on the amount she can invest. With her income and net worth, she falls within subsection (i). That means she can invest up to $7,500—which is the greater of $2,500 or 5% of $150,000.

Required Disclosure Document. Issuers must provide investors with an Offering Circular prior to the start of the offering. *See* Regulation Crowdfunding § 227.201. Although not as exhaustive as the disclosures that an issuer would be required to make in a registered offering, the disclosures in the Offering Circular are fairly demanding. For example, the issuer is required to disclose information about the company's business, business plan, financial condition, management team, ownership structure, risk factors, and the use of proceeds. In addition, if the issuer raised more than $124,000 through the exemption, the issuer must include financial statements reviewed by an independent public accountant. If the issuer raised more than $618,000, those financial statements might have to be audited by an independent public accountant. If the numbers seem strange, they are. It's because Congress provided for adjustments for inflation.

SEC Filing Requirements. The issuer must file an Offering Statement on Form C with the SEC when the offering begins. *See* Regulation Crowdfunding § 227.204(a) of Regulation Crowdfunding.

Limitations on the Manner of Offering. All crowdfunding offerings must be made through an intermediary that uses an Internet-based platform. *See* Securities Act of 1933 § 4A. These funding portals must be registered with the SEC. The intermediary provides a variety of services, including making a communications channel available to potential investors so that they can communicate about the crowdfunding offering. That's the wisdom of the crowd idea. The intermediary is also required to take certain steps to reduce the risk of fraud.

Before filing the Form C with the SEC, the issuer can test the waters to see if there are interested investors. *See* Regulation

Crowdfunding § 227.206. After the Form C has been filed, the issuer can advertise freely on the intermediary's platform. Outside of the platform, the issuer can only advertise through a notice that directs investors to the platform. *See* Regulation Crowdfunding § 227.204.

Resale Restrictions. In general, purchasers can't resell securities acquired in a crowdfunding offering for at least one year. *See* Regulation Crowdfunding § 227.501.

Ongoing SEC Reporting Requirements. An issuer that sells securities through the crowdfunding exemption must file a Form C-Annual Report with the SEC at the end of the company's fiscal year. *See* Regulation Crowdfunding § 227.204(b).

F. Regulation A

Regulation A is often referred to as "mini-registration" or a "mini-IPO." That's because Regulation A requires the issuer to file with the SEC a disclosure document—a Form 1-A—that resembles (though in simplified form) a Registration Statement on Form S-1 that's used in registered offerings. Moreover, the Form 1-A is subject to SEC comment, and the issuer must receive SEC approval before sales can begin. While these may be seen as drawbacks, there are some advantages to using Reg A, including that there are no investor eligibility requirements, meaning that sales can be made to the public. In addition, there are no resale restrictions, so investors can immediately resell their securities.

While Reg A may resemble registration, it *is* an exemption. And it exempts two types of offerings: Tier 1 Offerings and Tier 2 Offerings.

1. Tier 1 Offerings

Tier 1 offerings can raise up to $20 million. In addition, there are other conditions:

Issuer Eligibility Requirements. Reg A can't be used by bad actors. *See* Securities Act of 1933 Rule 251(b).

Limitations on Offering Amount. Issuers can raise up to $20 million in any 12-month period. *See* Securities Act of 1933 Rule 251(a)(1).

Required Disclosure Document. The issuer must provide purchasers with an Offering Circular, which is required to include most of the information that's set forth in the Form 1-A. The Offering Circular contains fairly detailed information about the company and the offering. It also must include two years of financial statements, although the financial statements don't have to be audited. *See* Securities Act of 1933 Rule 253.

SEC Filing Requirements. The issuer must file a Form 1-A with the SEC. The SEC will review and comment on the Form 1-A. When the SEC is satisfied with the disclosure, it will "qualify" the offering, which means that the issuer can start selling securities. *See* Securities Act of 1933 Rule 251(d)(2).

Limitations on the Manner of Offering. Prior to the qualification of the offering, the issuer can test the waters to gauge investor interest in the offering. *See* Securities Act of 1933 Rule 251(d)(1). After qualification, the issuer can engage in advertising and general solicitation.

2. *Tier 2 Offerings*

Tier 2 offerings can raise up to $75 million. In addition, there are other conditions:

Issuer Eligibility Requirements. Reg A can't be used by bad actors. *See* Securities Act of 1933 Rule 251(b).

Limitations on Offering Amount. Issuers can raise up to $75 million in any 12-month period. *See* Securities Act of 1933 Rule 251(a)(2).

Limitations on Investment Amount. Accredited investors can purchase as much as they want in a Tier 2 offering. Non-accredited investors, however, face limits on the amount they can purchase. Specifically, they can't purchase more than 10% of the greater of their annual income or net worth. *See* Securities Act of 1933 Rule 251(d)(2).

Required Disclosure Document. The issuer must provide purchasers with an Offering Circular, which is required to include most of the information that's set forth in the Form 1-A. The Offering Circular contains fairly detailed information about the company and the offering. It also must include two years of financial statements, although the financial statements don't have to be audited. *See* Securities Act of 1933 Rule 253.

SEC Filing Requirements. The issuer must file a Form 1-A with the SEC. The SEC will review and comment on the Form 1-A. When the SEC is satisfied with the disclosure, it will "qualify" the offering, which means that the issuer can start selling securities. *See* Securities Act of 1933 Rule 251(d)(2).

Limitations on the Manner of Offering. Prior to the qualification of the offering, the issuer can test the waters to gauge investor interest in the offering. *See* Securities Act of 1933 Rule

251(d)(1). After qualification, the issuer can engage in advertising and general solicitation.

Ongoing SEC Reporting Requirements. Following a Tier 2 offering, issuers are required to file annual reports, quarterly reports, and current reports with the SEC. *See* Securities Act of 1933 Rule 257(b). This is a drawback to using this exemption.

G. Integration

Companies, especially start-ups, often engage in multiple rounds of financing. In other words, an issuer might sell $5 million of securities through Rule 147A and then sell $10 million of securities the following month through Rule 506(c). The question that arises in these cases is whether these are really two separate offerings, or whether the two offerings are, in fact, one offering. Why does it matter? It matters because the issuer might not have been able to find one exemption that would allow it to raise $15 million, so the issuer carved the offering up into two offerings. The SEC views this as an improper way to avoid registration. To prevent it, the SEC created the "integration doctrine."

If the integration doctrine applies, two seemingly separate offerings will be combined into one offering. If this happens, neither exemption will probably be available. Think of the above example. The Rule 147A offering probably included non-accredited investors, and the Rule 506(c) offering probably included investors living in multiple states. Thus, the Rule 147A exemption will be blown, and the Rule 506(c) exemption will be blown. This means that the issuer sold securities in violation of Section 5.

How do we know whether offerings will be integrated? Rule 152 tells us. It's a complicated rule, but there are three important take-aways that you should be particularly aware of.

First, according to Rule 152(a), offerings will not be integrated if the issuer can show that an exemption is available for each offering. This makes sense. If an exemption is available for each offering, then the justifications supporting each exemption are valid. When might an exemption not be available for each offering? Typically this happens when an offering made pursuant to an exemption that doesn't allow advertising and general solicitation follows an offering made pursuant to an exemption that does allow it.

For example, think of a Rule 506(b) offering following a Rule 147A offering. The advertising and general solicitation used in the Rule 147A offering might have reached the purchasers in the Rule 506(b) offering, which would blow the exemption. If that happens, the offerings will be integrated—unless the issuer can show that the advertising and general solicitation didn't reach the purchasers in the Rule 506(b) offering or that the issuer had already established a substantive relationship with the purchasers in the Rule 506(b) offering prior to the start of the Rule 506(b) offering. *See* Securities Act of 1933 Rule 152(a)(1).

Second, Rule 152(b) includes several safe harbors, including a 30-day bright line safe harbor, which provides that any offering made more than 30 calendar days before the start of any other offering, or more than 30 calendar days after the termination or completion of any other offering, won't be integrated with the other offering. Unfortunately, this safe harbor doesn't apply to the situation described in the previous paragraph. That means, for example, that even if a Rule 147A and a Rule 506(b) offering are more than 30 days apart, the safe harbor won't help. You'll have to do the facts and circumstances approach described in the previous paragraph. *See* Securities Act of 1933 Rule 152(b)(1).

Finally, Rule 152 addresses not just the possible integration of two or more exempt offerings. It also addresses integration of exempt offerings and a registered offering. Rule 152(b)(3) includes a safe harbor that provides that that a registered offering won't be integrated if the Registration Statement is filed after:

- A terminated or completed offering for which general solicitation is not permitted;
- A terminated or completed offering for which general solicitation is permitted and made only to qualified institutional buyers (QIBs) and institutional accredited investors (IAIs); or
- An offering for which general solicitation is permitted that terminated or was completed more than 30 days prior to the commencement of the registered offering.

H. Summary Charts

As promised, the following charts summarize the requirements of each exemption:

Summary of the Private Placement Exemption and Regulation D

	Section 4(a)(2): Private Placement	Reg D: Rule 504	Reg D: Rule 506(b)	Reg D: Rule 506(c)
Issuer Eligibility Requirements	None	Non-reporting issuers only; no bad actors.	No bad actors	No bad actors
Limitation on Offering Amount	None	$10 million	None	None

Limitation on Number of Purchasers	None	None	35, not including accredited investors	None
Limitation on Investment Amount	None	None	None	None
Required Disclosure Document	Offerees must receive private placement memo or have effective access to info	None	Yes, if any sales made to non-accredited investors	None
Investor Qualification Requirements	Offerees must be sophisticated	None	Investors must be accredited or sophisticated	Investors must be verified accredited investors
Limitations on Manner of Offering	Ban on advertising and general solicitation	Ban on advertising and general solicitation, with three exceptions	Ban on advertising and general solicitation	None
Resale Restrictions	Yes	Yes, with three exceptions	Yes	Yes
SEC Filing Requirements	None	Issuer must file a Form D	Issuer must file a Form D	Issuer must file a Form D

Ongoing SEC Reporting Requirements	None	None	None	None

Summary of the Intrastate Offering Exemptions

	Intrastate Offering: Section 3(a)(11)	**Intrastate Offering: Rule 147**	**Intrastate Offering: Rule 147A**
Issuer Eligibility Requirements	Issuer must be "resident" and "doing business" in a single state; residence = state of incorporation	Issuer must be "resident" and "doing business" in a single state; residence = state of incorporation and principal place of business	Issuer must be "resident" and "doing business" in a single state; residence = state of principal place of business
Limitation on Offering Amount	None	None	None
Limitation on Number of Purchasers	None	None	None
Limitation on Investment Amount	None	None	None
Required Disclosure Document	None	None	None
Investor Qualification Requirements	All offerees and purchasers must be	All offerees and purchasers must be "resident" in a	All purchasers must be "resident" in

	"resident" in a single state; residence = domicile	single state; residence = principal residence	a single state; residence = principal residence
Limitations on Manner of Offering	Must be consistent with intrastate character of exemption	Must be consistent with intrastate character of exemption	None
Resale Restrictions	No resales to non-residents until offering has "come to rest"	No sales to non-residents for six months	No resales to non-residents for six months
SEC Filing Requirements	None	None	None
Ongoing SEC Reporting Requirements	None	None	None

Summary of Crowdfunding and Regulation A

	Crowdfunding: Section 4(a)(6) and Regulation CF	**Regulation A: Tier 1 Rule 251**	**Regulation A: Tier 2 Rule 251**
Issuer Eligibility Requirements	Non-reporting issuers only	No bad actors	No bad actors
Limitation on Offering Amount	$5 million	$20 million	$75 million
Limitation on Number of Purchasers	None	None	None

Limitation on Investment Amount	Non-accredited investors are limited on how much they can invest, depending on annual income and net worth	None	Non-accredited investors can't invest more than 10% of greater of annual income or net worth
Required Disclosure Document	Purchasers must receive an Offering Circular	Purchasers must receive an Offering Circular	Purchasers must receive an Offering Circular
Investor Qualification Requirements	None	None	None
Limitations on Manner of Offering	Purchases must be made through funding portal Before Form C filed, testing the waters is permitted After Form C filed, advertising can only be done through funding portal	Sales can't be made until offering is qualified by SEC Before offering qualified, testing the waters is permitted After offering is qualified, advertising and general solicitation is permitted	Sales can't be made until offering is qualified by SEC Before offering qualified, testing the waters is permitted After offering is qualified, advertising and general solicitation is permitted
Resale Restrictions	No resales for 12 months	None	None

SEC Filing Requirements	Issuer must file a Form C	Issuer must file a Form 1-A	Issuer must file a Form 1-A
Ongoing SEC Reporting Requirements	Issuer must file a Form C-AR each year	None	Issuer must file annual, quarterly, and current reports

I. Quick Recap

Exemptions permit companies to offer and sell securities without having to register the offering with the SEC. So you should think of exemptions as your friend. A complicated and high maintenance friend, maybe, but a good friend nonetheless. If you get lost in the weeds, remember that each exemption's conditions reflect a balancing of two policies: protecting investors and helping companies raise capital.

Hopefully, the summary charts will help you determine whether an exemption is available for an offering. And remember that there are two especially important issues to your exemption analysis: accredited investor status and restrictions on advertising and general solicitation.

CHAPTER 6

Resales of Securities

A. Introduction

The '33 Act doesn't just regulate sales by issuers. It also regulates resales of securities by investors. That's because Section 5 prohibits "any person" from selling securities unless the offering has been registered with the SEC or unless an exemption from registration is available. Fortunately, there are several exemptions that permit investors to resell their securities. The primary resale exemption is Section 4(a)(1), commonly referred to as the trading transaction exemption. However, most resales are made pursuant to Rule 144, which is the safe harbor for Section 4(a)(1). In addition, although uncommon, some resales are made outside of Rule 144. Each of these exemptions is discussion below.

B. The Section 4(a)(1) Trading Transaction Exemption

Section 4(a)(1) is intended to exempt trading transactions—*i.e.*, resales made by investors on a stock exchange. If you think about it, this exemption makes perfect sense. The purpose of the '33 Act is to regulate offerings by issuers. It's the job of the '34 Act to regulate what happens after securities are in the hands of investors.

Section 4(a)(1) exempts "transactions by any person other than an issuer, underwriter, or dealer." With resales, the key question is whether an underwriter is involved. Fortunately, the '33 Act defines "underwriter." According to Section 2(a)(11), an underwriter is:

- Any person who has purchased from an issuer with a view to distribution; or
- Any person who offers or sells for an issuer in connection with a distribution.[1]

The first definition of underwriter can be broken down into three elements. An underwriter is any person:

1. Who has purchased securities from an issuer
2. With a view to quickly reselling the securities
3. In a distribution.

The second definition can also be broken down into three elements. An underwriter is any person:

1. Who offers or sells securities
2. For an issuer
3. In connection with a distribution.

Both of these definitions capture the kinds of traditional underwriters we discussed in Chapter 3. For example, assume that Goldman Sachs is retained to conduct a firm commitment underwriting. Goldman Sachs falls within the definition of an underwriter under Section 2(a)(11) because it (1) purchased securities from an issuer (2) with a view to quickly reselling the

[1] Section 2(a)(11) includes two additional definitions of underwriter. However, they aren't typically used. The first two definitions are the important ones, and that's what we'll focus on.

securities (3) in a distribution. "Distribution" isn't defined in the federal securities laws, but courts have determined that it is equivalent to a public offering. Similarly, if an investment bank conducted a best-efforts underwriting, it will fall within the second definition of underwriter. That's because the investment bank (1) offered securities (2) for an issuer (3) in connection with a distribution.

But the definition of "underwriter" isn't limited to investment banks, and that creates several resale issues.

1. Resale Issue #1: Inadvertent Underwriters

Regular investors—people like you and me—might become underwriters, even if we didn't intend to. For example, think of an investor who purchased securities from an issuer in a private placement and then immediately resold them on a stock exchange. This investor (1) purchased securities from an issuer (2) with a view to quickly reselling the securities (3) in a distribution. A sale on a stock exchange constitutes a "distribution" because the securities are being offered to the public. Since all three elements of the first definition of underwriter are met, the investor becomes an underwriter, and the Section 4(a)(1) exemption won't be available for the investor's resale.

So how can regular investors resell securities without violating Section 5? Most investors want to resell their securities on a stock exchange—which constitutes a distribution, one of the three elements of the definition of underwriter. That means the way to do it would be to avoid meeting one of the other two elements. Thus, for example, if the investor initially purchased the securities on a stock exchange, the investor wouldn't have "purchased from an issuer." Therefore, the investor isn't an underwriter and would be able to use Section 4(a)(1) to resell the securities on a securities exchange.

If the investor did purchase the securities from the issuer, the answer turns on whether the investor intended to quickly resell the securities. If he did, then he might be an underwriter. On the other hand, if, at the time the investor purchased the securities, the investor intended to keep the securities for an indefinite length of time, then the second prong won't be met. This is referred to as "investment intent." If investment intent exists, the investor won't be an underwriter.

How do we know whether the investor purchased with investment intent? The best evidence of investment intent is the length of time the investor actually held on to the securities before reselling them. This is referred to as the "holding period." In general, a holding period of three years conclusively establishes investment intent. A holding period of less than a year means that the investor won't be able to establish investment intent. If the holding period is between one year and three years, the investor might be able to show investment intent. It'll be a facts and circumstances analysis of the investor's intentions at the time he purchased the securities. Hopefully, your professor won't be so cruel on the exam.

2. Resale Issue #2: Resales by Control Persons

Resales by "control persons" create a different resale issue. A control person is someone who has the power to direct the issuer. *See* Securities Act of 1933 Rule 405. Examples of control persons include controlling stockholders, directors, and executive officers of the issuer.

Look at the last sentence of Section 2(a)(11)—the definition of underwriter. It states that "[a]s used in this paragraph the term 'issuer' shall include, in addition to an issuer, any person directly or indirectly controlling or controlled by the issuer or any person under direct or indirect common control with the issuer." This means, for example, that when a control person resells securities, an underwriter is any person:

1. Who offers or sells securities

2. For an issuer *or control person*

3. In connection with a distribution.

Since a broker is always involved in the resale of securities on a stock exchange, the broker becomes an underwriter. That's because the broker is (1) offering or selling securities (2) for a control person (3) in connection with a distribution. Remember that a sale on a stock exchange constitutes a distribution.

The effect of the last sentence of Section 2(a)(11) is that a control person can't use Section 4(a)(1) to resell securities on a stock exchange. Even if the control person isn't an underwriter, the control person can't rely on Section 4(a)(1) because the *broker* is an underwriter.

Think about that for a second. A control person might've purchased stock from the issuer in a private placement ten years ago—meaning that the control person has established investment intent—so the control person isn't an underwriter. But the control person can't rely on Section 4(a)(1) to resell the stock on a stock exchange because the broker is an underwriter. Or the control person might've purchased stock in the issuer on a stock exchange—meaning that the control person didn't "purchase from an issuer"—so the control person isn't an underwriter. But, once again, the control person can't rely on Section 4(a)(1) to resell the stock on a stock exchange because the broker is an underwriter. Obviously, this creates a real problem for control persons wanting to resell their securities.

Why did Congress effectively make it impossible for control persons to resell their securities on an exchange? The answer is that Congress was concerned that a control person's resale was really a disguised public offering by the issuer. Therefore, Congress wanted the control person's securities to be sold through a registered offering. And because the control person by definition has "control" over the issuer, the control person would be able to use its power to compel the company to register the offering for sale to the public.

Fortunately, as we'll see, Rule 144 permits control persons to resell their securities on an exchange if certain conditions are met.

3. Resale Issue #3: Resales of Securities Purchased in Registered Offerings

Most resale issues involve securities sold through exemptions, but we don't want to overlook sales made through registered offerings. Fortunately, if an investor—a control person or a non-control person—purchased securities from an issuer in a registered offering and wants to immediately resell the securities, that's perfectly okay. We don't have to worry about whether Section 4(a)(1) is available to exempt the resale. That's because the *offering* has been registered, so no exemption from Section 5 is needed. The offering includes not just the initial sale of securities by the issuer, but all resales until the offering has concluded. Securities lawyers refer to the conclusion of an offering as "coming to rest." Most practitioners would agree that an offer has come to rest after one year.

If the resale occurs after the registered offering comes to rest, an investor who is not a control person can use Section 4(a)(1) to resell the securities on an exchange. That's because the non-control person will be able to establish investment intent. That means the resale didn't involve an underwriter, and Section 4(a)(1) will be available.

It's different story for control persons wanting to resell securities after the registered offering has come to rest. That's because, as discussed above, while the control person won't be an underwriter because investment intent has been established, the broker helping the control person resell securities on a stock exchange becomes an underwriter. That means that Section 4(a)(1) won't be available for the resale.

Once again, as we'll see, Rule 144 will come to the rescue for the control person.

C. Resales Under Rule 144

In practice, the starting point for a resale analysis is Rule 144, the safe harbor for Section 4(a)(1). Like all safe harbors, Rule 144 provides more bright line rules for planners. Rule 144 states that if the conditions of the rule are met, the person shall be "deemed not to be an underwriter" of those securities. If there's no underwriter involved in the resale, then Section 4(a)(1) is available.

Rule 144 doesn't apply to all resales. It protects three types of resales:

1. Resales of restricted securities by a non-control person [resale of restricted securities];
2. Resales of restricted securities by a control person or person selling on behalf of a control person [resale of restricted control securities]; and
3. Resales of non-restricted securities by a person selling on behalf of a control person [resale of control securities].

That means we need to understand the terms "restricted securities" and "control person."

Rule 144(a)(3) provides a list of "restricted securities" that includes securities sold pursuant to the following exemptions:

- Section 4(a)(2) private placement exemption

- Rule 504—if the sale is subject to resale restrictions [*See* Securities Act of 1933 Rule 502(d) and Rule 504(b)(1)]
- Rule 506(b)
- Rule 506(c)

That means that restricted securities don't include securities offered in registered offerings, as well as securities sold pursuant to the following exemptions:

- Rule 504—if the sale isn't subject to resale restrictions [*See* Rule 502(d) and Rule 504(b)(1)]
- Section 3(a)(11)
- Rule 147 and Rule 147A
- Regulation A
- Regulation Crowdfunding

"Control person" has the same meaning as the term is used in the definition of "underwriter." In other words, it includes controlling shareholders, directors, and executive officers of the issuer. Note that while Rule 144 uses the term "affiliate," affiliate has the same meaning as a "control person."

Each of the three types of resales covered by Rule 144 have different conditions that must be met.

1. Resale of Restricted Securities by a Non-Control Person

Rule 144 makes it very easy for non-control persons reselling restricted securities. Unlike resales under Section 4(a)(1), there's no need to determine "investment intent." Instead, there is a holding period requirement.

For reporting companies, the holding period is six months. That means that non-control persons can resell stock in a reporting company on an exchange after owning the stock for only six months. However, if the non-control person is reselling restricted securities after holding them for six months but before one year has elapsed, there is one additional requirement: current public information must be available about the reporting company. "Current public information" means the issuer has filed its annual report on Form 10-K and its quarterly reports on Form 10-Qs with the SEC during the 12 months preceding the sale (or for such shorter period that the issuer was required to file periodic reports). After one year, the non-control person can freely resell the restricted securities, even if current public information isn't available about the company.

If it's a non-reporting company, there is a one-year holding period, and no other conditions attach.

This might seem confusing, so let's go through an example. First, let's assume that Nancy, a non-control person, purchased stock sold in a private placement by BigCo, Inc., a public company. Eight months have passed, and Nancy wants to resell the stock. Can she use Rule 144?

The first question you should ask is whether Rule 144 is even available. Nancy is a non-control person, so Rule 144 is only available for her if she is reselling restricted securities. Because the stock was sold pursuant to Section 4(a)(2), it's a restricted security. This means that Rule 144 is potentially available for Nancy's resale.

Next, you need to determine the appropriate holding period. Since the issuer is a reporting company, the holding period is six months. Since Nancy has held for eight months, the holding period is met. However, because Nancy hasn't held for at least a year, Rule 144 imposes the current public information condition on this resale. If the company has filed its periodic reports with the SEC in the last year, then Nancy can rely on Rule 144 to resell her securities.

If the company missed the deadline for its most recent Form 10-Q, the current public information requirement wouldn't be met, which means that Nancy couldn't use Rule 144. However, all is not lost for Nancy. If she waits a few more months, so that her holding period is a year, she would be able to freely resell under Rule 144.

Put another way, non-control persons can freely resell restricted securities with no other conditions if they have held them for at least a year.

2. *Resale of Restricted Securities by a Control Person*

While Rule 144 certainly benefits non-control persons, control persons are the rule's biggest beneficiaries. That's because Rule 144 is the only way that control persons can resell securities on a stock exchange.

When control persons are reselling restricted securities, Rule 144 imposes five conditions. First, since these are restricted securities, there's a holding period requirement: six months (for the resale of the stock of public companies) or one year (for the resale of stock of non-reporting companies). *See* Securities Act of 1933 Rule 144(d).

Second, there's a current public information requirement. If the issuer is a public company, the issuer must've filed the Form 10-K and all Form 10-Qs required during the 12 months preceding the sale (or for such shorter period that the issuer was required to file periodic reports). If the issuer isn't a reporting company, information similar to the Form 10-K must be publicly available. *See* Securities Act of 1933 Rule 144(c).

Third, there are volume limitations, which prevent the control person from dumping large quantities of stock on a stock exchange. Specifically, the amount of stock that can be resold in any three-month period is limited to the greater of either (1) 1% of the issuer's outstanding stock; or (2) the average weekly trading volume of the issuer's securities. *See* Securities Act of 1933 Rule 144(c). *See* Securities Act of 1933 Rule 144(e).

Fourth, there is a manner of sale requirement. *See* Securities Act of 1933 Rule 144(f). In general, this means that the resales must be made through a "broker's transaction," defined as an unsolicited transaction where the broker simply executes the customer's order and receives the standard broker's commission. *See* Securities Act of 1933 Rule 144(g).

Finally, there is a notice filing requirement. If the control person is selling more than 5,000 shares of than $50,000 worth of stock, the resale must be disclosed to the SEC through a Form 144 filing. *See* Securities Act of 1933 Rule 144(h).

Let's run through a quick example. Let's assume that Pooja is the Chief Executive Officer of a BigCo, Inc., a public company. Since it went public, BigCo has timely filed all of its periodic reports with the SEC. 30 million shares of BigCo stock are outstanding, and its stock trades on the New York Stock Exchange. The average weekly trading volume is 600,000 shares. Ten years ago, Pooja purchased 500,000 shares of BigCo stock in a Rule 506(b) offering. Last month, she sold 100,000 of these shares on the NYSE pursuant to Rule 144; she hasn't sold any other shares in the last year. Can she rely on Rule 144 to resell another 200,000 shares this month?

The first thing for you to do is determine whether Pooja is a control person of BigCo. As the CEO of BigCo, she meets the definition.

The next thing to do is determine if the securities are restricted or non-restricted securities. Securities sold pursuant to Rule 506(b) are restricted securities. Rule 144 is potentially available for Pooja's resale.

Rule 144 places five conditions on a control person's resale of restricted securities. First, the holding period requirement is six months—because BigCo is a public company. Pooja has held for ten years, so she easily meets the holding period condition. Second, the current public information requirement has been met because the facts state that BigCo has timely filed its Form 10-K and Form 10-Qs for the last 12 months. Third, the volume limitation has been met. Pooja can sell in any three-month period the greater of 300,000 shares (1% of 30 million) of 600,000 shares. Thus, the volume limitation is 600,000 shares. Since she sold 100,000 shares last month, she can use Rule 144 to resell up to 500,000 shares this month. 200,000 shares is less than 500,000 shares, so we're good. Fourth, the sale must be made through a broker's transaction. If Pooja's sale was made through a broker, who simply executed the order, then the condition is met. Finally, since Pooja's sale of 200,000 shares exceeds 5,000 shares, she must make a Form 144 notice filing with the SEC.

3. Resale of Non-Restricted Securities by a Control Person

When a control person is selling non-restricted securities, the conditions are very similar to the conditions imposed on a control person selling restricted securities. However, there is one significant difference: there is no holding period requirement. Thus, there are four conditions: (1) current public information; (2) volume limitations; (3) manner of sale; and (4) Rule 144 filing.

D. Resales Made Outside of Rule 144

While most resales are made pursuant to Rule 144, what if it can't be used? There are three other ways:

1. Section 4(1-1/2) Exemption

In practice, most resales are made using Rule 144. However, sometimes Rule 144 isn't available. Maybe a control person wants to sell more securities than permitted by Rule 144's volume limitation. Or maybe the company didn't file its periodic reports with the SEC. When this happens, the reseller may be forced to rely on the so-called Section 4(1-1/2) exemption. In a Section 4(1-1/2) transaction, the resale is made privately, not on an exchange.

Obviously, the '33 Act doesn't include a Section 4(1-1/2) exemption. The actual exemption that's being used is Section 4(a)(1). Lawyers refer to private resales as 4(1-1/2) transactions because we're relying on cases interpreting Section 4(a)(2) to determine if the sale was "private." In effect, Section 4(a)(2) is being merged with Section 4(a)(1), giving us Section 4(1-1/2).

How does this work? Let's run through an example. Bill is a control person of BigCo who wants to sell resell 1,000,000 shares of BigCo stock that he purchased from BigCo five years ago in a Rule 506(b) offering. Rule 144 isn't available because the number of shares exceeds Rule 144's volume limitations. So Bill hires an investment bank to find a purchaser for his stock. The investment back contacts one of its clients, Rachel, who is a sophisticated and wealthy investor. Rachel is provided with a disclosure document containing information similar to what she would receive in a registered offering. Bill sells his stock to Rachel. Section 4(1-1/2)—really, Section 4(a)(1)—is available for this resale. Why? Because there are no underwriters involved.

Remember that the definition of underwriter requires a distribution, and "distribution" has been defined to mean "public offering." Because the resale was made privately—to someone who would've met Section 4(a)(2)'s *Ralson-Purina* test—there is no public offering. No public offering, no distribution, no underwriter, no resale problem.

2. *Section 4(a)(7)*

Section 4(a)(7) exempts certain private resales of securities. In general, it permits resales to accredited investors when no general solicitation is used. We discussed the definition of accredited investor and general solicitation in Chapter 5. Basically, Section 4(a)(7) is safe harbor for the Section 4(1-1/2) exemption.

3. *Rule 144A*

Rule 144A exempts certain private resales of securities. It can be used to resell securities to "qualified institutional buyers." In general, QIBs are institutional investors that oversee investments of at least $100 million. However, Rule 144A can't be used to resell securities that are traded on a securities exchange. Thus, Rule 144A is typically used to resell preferred stock and debt issued in private placements.

E. Quick Recap

An investor can't resell securities unless an exemption from Section 5 is available. The main exemption is Section 4(a)(1), which exempts trading transactions from Section 5. The key to resales is identifying whether an underwriter is involved in the resale. If an underwriter is involved, it's not a trading transaction, and Section 4(a)(1) won't be available.

Non-control persons usually have no problems reselling securities. Control persons, on the other hand, won't be able to rely on Section 4(a)(1) to resell their stock on a stock exchange. That's because (1) anyone who offers or sells securities (2) for a control person (3) in connection with a distribution becomes an underwriter. Put another way, a broker executing a control person's sell order on an exchange becomes an underwriter. Therefore, Section 4(a)(1) won't be available.

But Rule 144 to the rescue! The SEC promulgated Rule 144 to make resales easier. In your Rule 144 analysis, make sure you determine whether the seller is a non-control person or a control person and whether the securities are restricted or un-restricted. This will help you identify the correct conditions that must be met for Rule 144 to apply.

CHAPTER 7

Liability Under the '33 Act

A. Introduction

As we know, the '33 Act is all about requiring companies to provide information to investors so that they can make informed investment decisions. But mandatory disclosure only works if accurate information is provided to investors. But what if it isn't? Or what if the information isn't accurate? That's where enforcement comes in.

The SEC can certainly enforce the '33 Act by suing violators. But the SEC doesn't have unlimited resources. So Congress expressly permitted investors to sue for violations of the '33 Act, creating a regime of private attorneys general.

There are four private rights of action under the '33 Act:

- Section 12(a)(1): for violations of Section 5—*i.e.*, if unregistered securities were sold without a valid exemption
- Section 11: for false or misleading statements in a registration statement

- Section 12(a)(2): for false or misleading statements in a prospectus
- Section 15: for anyone who "controls" a person who violated the '33 Act

B. Section 12(a)(1): Violations of Section 5

As we know, Section 5 is the heart of the'33 Act. It effectuates the investor protection goals of the federal securities laws by creating the registration process. Section 12(a)(1) permits investors to sue for violations of Section 5.

There are only two elements to a Section 12(a)(1) claim:

1. An offer or sale of a security
2. Made in violation of Section 5: i.e., when the when the issuer "jumps the gun" during the offering process, as explained in Chapter 4, or when securities are sold without registration and without a valid exemption.

That's it. There are no other elements. Congress wanted to scare companies into complying with Section 5 by making it easy for plaintiffs to sue. Note that plaintiffs don't have to establish negligence, let alone scienter, under Section 12(a)(1). It provides for strict liability.

That means, for example, if an issuer made an unregistered sale of securities pursuant to Regulation D, but it turned out that Regulation D wasn't available, purchasers could sue the issuer under Section 12(a)(1) for rescission or rescissory damages. The purchasers could require the issuer to give them their money back—which could be devastating for the issuer.

Who can the plaintiff sue under Section 12(a)(1)? The so-called "statutory seller." According to the Supreme Court, there are two types of statutory sellers: (1) the person who passed title to the securities to the plaintiff; and (2) any person who "successfully solicits the purchase, motivated at least in part by a desire to serve his own financial interests or those of the [issuer]." *See* Pinter v. Dahl, 486 U.S. 622 (1988). The second definition means that plaintiffs can ordinarily sue the brokers or promoters of an offering that was made in violation of Section 5.

C. Section 11: False or Misleading Statements in a Registration Statement

Section 12(a)(1) helps ensure that investors receive information before they purchase securities from an issuer, but it doesn't address the accuracy of the information provided. That's where Section 11 comes in. It states that "[i]n case any part of the registration statement, when such part became effective, contained an untrue statement of a material fact or omitted to state a material fact required to be stated therein or necessary to make the statements therein not misleading, any person acquiring such security . . . may . . . sue [certain enumerated defendants]." *See* Securities Act of 1933 § 11.

Breaking this down, the elements of a Section 11 action are:

1. The sale of a security
2. By means of a Registration Statement
3. That contains a false or misleading statement of material fact on the date of effectiveness

The first thing to notice is that Section 11 only applies to *registered* offerings. This means, for example, that Section 11 doesn't apply if there were false or misleading statements appearing in an Offering Circular used in a Regulation D transaction.

Second, truth or falsity is tested on the effective date of the Registration Statement. This means that post-effective developments aren't actionable under Section 11. For example, assume that a Registration Statement stated that the company had 10 million subscribers, and this was true on the effective date of February 5th. However, the company lost 2 million subscribers after February 5th. An investor who purchased stock after February 5th—when the company had only 8 million subscribers—wouldn't be able to bring a claim under Section 11 because the Registration Statement was accurate on February 5th.

Who can sue under Section 11? Courts have held that plaintiffs must be able to trace the securities they purchased back to the false or misleading Registration Statement. This means that Section 11 won't be much help to investors who purchased in a registered offering made by a company that's already public. Stock is fungible. The stock purchased by these investors could've been issued pursuant to the false or misleading Registration Statement or the stock it could've been issued pursuant to a Registration Statement that was filed years ago. Effectively, this means that Section 11 is used primarily by plaintiffs purchasing stock in an IPO.

Not everyone involved in preparing the Registration Statement can be sued under Section 11. Section 11 provides a list of enumerated defendants:

- The issuer
- The issuer's board of directors
- The issuer's Chief Executive Office, Chief Financial Officer, and Chief Accounting Officer
- The underwriters
- The accounting firm that audited the issuer's financial statements—but only with respect to the financial statements they prepared

While this list includes most of the major players in a public offering, it doesn't include the lawyers who drafted and approved the Registration Statement.

Although Section 11 reads like a fraud claim, Section 11 is much easier to prove than common law fraud. That was by design. Congress wanted to scare these potential defendants into doing everything they could do to ensure that the information in the Registration Statement was accurate. The following chart shows the important differences in the required elements:

Elements of Common Law Fraud	**Elements of Section 11**
False or Misleading Statement of Material Fact	Yes
Transaction Causation/Reliance	No
Loss Causation	No (but lack of loss causation is an affirmative defense)
Scienter	No

The most notable difference is that a Section 11 plaintiff doesn't have to prove that the defendant intended to deceive investors. In fact, the issuer is strictly liable under Section 11. Think about that! The issuer is essentially the guarantor of the accuracy of the Registration Statement. All other Section 11 defendants have a "due diligence" defense.

In general, to rely on the due diligence defense, non-issuer defendants must first conduct a "reasonable investigation." Then they must show that, following this reasonable investigation, they actually and reasonably believed that the information in the Registration Statement was true. *See* Securities Act of 1933

§ 11(b)(3)(A) and § 11(b)(3)(B). Put another way, this means that a defendant won't have a due diligence defense if:

- There was no investigation, or the investigation wasn't reasonable;
- The defendant didn't have reasonable grounds to believe that the statement was true; or
- The defendant knew that that statement wasn't true.

"Reasonableness" isn't a one-size-fits-all standard. It's often referred to as a "sliding scale." *See* Securities Act of 1933 Rule 176. That means, for example, that it might be reasonable for an outside director to have believed that certain information in the Registration Statement was true, but not for an inside director—who is way more knowledgeable about the company and its affairs.

While the due diligence defense generally requires the defendant to conduct an investigation, there is one situation when a reasonable investigation isn't required: When the false or misleading statement appears in the "expertised" section of the Registration Statement and the defendant is a "non-expert." *See* Securities Act of 1933 § 11(b)(3)(C). An expertised section is a part of the Registration Statement that was prepared by an expert, such as the financial statements (prepared by accountants) or legal opinions (provided by attorneys). In this case, the non-expert isn't required to conduct an investigation to sustain the due diligence defense. The non-expert is allowed to rely on the expert's work—unless it wouldn't be reasonable to do so. When you think about it, this qualified right to rely on the work of an expert makes sense. If the non-expert were required to conduct a reasonable investigation, the non-expert would need to hire a second expert to check the work of the first expert. This would add significant additional costs to the registration process.

So when will a non-expert be liable for false statements in an expertised portion of the Registration Statement, such as the financial statements? If there was a red flag that put the non-expert on notice that that the financial statements were false or if the non-expert actually knew that the financial statements were false.

D. Section 12(a)(2): False or Misleading Statements in a Prospectus

While Section 11 addresses false or misleading statements appearing in a Registration Statement, Section 12(a)(2) addresses false or misleading statements appearing in a prospectus. Under Section 12(a)(2), a purchaser can sue his "statutory seller" for rescission.

There are four elements to a Section 12(a)(2) claim:

1. An offer or sale of a security
2. By means of a prospectus (or oral communication relating to the prospectus)
3. That contains a false or misleading statement of material fact
4. That the plaintiff was not aware of.

Note that the plaintiff doesn't have to plead or prove scienter, transaction causation/reliance, or loss causation. The burden to disprove these elements is on the defendant. For example, Section 12(a)(2) provides that the defendant can escape liability by showing that "he did not know, and in the exercise of reasonable care could not have known, of such untruth or omission"—which the courts have interpreted to be a due diligence defense similar to the Section 11 due diligence defense. Alternatively, the defendant can also escape liability by showing a lack of loss causation. *See* Securities Act of 1933 § 12(b).

There are two significant issues with Section 12(a)(2). First, what's a "prospectus?" While the term is defined broadly in Section 2(a)(10), the Supreme Court has adopted a much more restrictive definition of "prospectus" for purposes of Section 12(a)(2). According to the Supreme Court, for purposes of Section 12(a)(2), "the word 'prospectus' is a term of art referring to a document that describes a public offering of securities by an issuer or controlling shareholder." *See* Gustafson v. Alloyd Co., 513 U.S. 561 (1995).

This means that Section 12(a)(2) can't be used if a false or misleading statement appears in a Private Placement Memorandum or a Regulation D Offering Circular—because these are not public offerings. Nor can Section 12(a)(2) be used if a false or misleading statement appears in a Stock Purchase Agreement. In fact, most commentators have interpreted the *Gustafson* case to mean that the term "prospectus" used in Section 12(a)(2) is limited to the formal prospectus that's part of the Registration Statement—the Section 10 prospectus discussed in Chapter 4.

Second, who can be sued? Unlike Section 11, Section 12(a)(2) doesn't include a list of enumerated defendants. Instead, according to Section 12(a)(2), plaintiffs can sue their "seller." The definition of seller is the same for both Section 12(a)(1) and Section 12(a)(2). As a reminder, there are two types of statutory sellers: (1) the person who passed title to the securities to the plaintiff; and (2) any person who "successfully solicits the purchase, motivated at least in part by a desire to serve his own financial interests or those of the [issuer]." *See* Pinter v. Dahl, 486 U.S. 622 (1988). Under the second definition of statutory seller, the investor would be able to sue any broker that encouraged the investor to purchase securities in the public offering.

But how does this work in a typical firm commitment public offering? Remember that in a firm commitment offering, the underwriter purchases securities from the issuer and then resells them to investors. That means that the underwriter, not the issuer, passes title to the securities to investors—which makes the underwriter a statutory seller. But the issuer doesn't get off the hook. That's because the SEC adopted a rule that expressly includes issuers as statutory sellers for purposes of Section 12(a)(2). *See* Securities Act of 1933 Rule 159A.

E. Control Person Liability

Liability doesn't stop with the person or company that violated the '33 Act. Under Section 15, "control persons" are liable for securities violations committed by someone else—even if the control person had nothing to do with the violation and even if the control person didn't even know about the violation. While it may not seem fair to the control person, this secondary liability reinforces the '33 Act's goals by extending liability to reach individuals who control the violators—and who therefore could presumably have prevented the violation from occurring in the first place. In addition, Section 15 provides the controlling person with a "good faith" defense. Specifically, the control person can escape liability if he "had no knowledge of or reasonable ground to believe in the existence" of the facts giving rise to the violation. *See* Securities Act of 1933 § 15(a).

Obviously, the big issue is establishing whether the defendant is a controlling person. Sometimes, the person's stock ownership, title, or job description establishes the necessary control. So, for example, majority stockholders are typically found to be controlling persons. And corporate officers have been found to be controlling persons over the employees they supervise. But courts have been hesitant to find directors to be controlling persons.

For additional discussion, see Chapter 11, which discusses control person liability under the '34 Act.

F. Quick Recap

In 1933, Congress recognized that it wasn't enough simply to require companies to disclose information to potential investors. It was just as important to ensure that companies actually follow through with providing accurate information to investors. That's why the '33 Act includes several express private rights of action which allow investors to bring lawsuits to enforce the federal securities laws. And some of these private rights of action contain provisions—such as strict liability for issuers—that make it easier for investors to recover. By enacting these "in terrorem" actions, Congress intended to scare issuers into providing accurate information to prevent the occurrence of another stock market crash.

CHAPTER 8

Public Companies and Periodic Reports

A. Introduction

Up to now, we've focused on the '33 Act—which seeks to ensure that investors can make informed choices about whether to buy securities from an issuer. But what about after the offering is over? And what about investors who purchase securities on an exchange—years after a public offering? Don't these investors need information to decide whether to hold their securities, sell their securities, or purchase more securities? That's where the '34 Act kicks in.

Among other things, the '34 Act requires public companies to disclose information to investors by filing periodic reports with the SEC: the annual report on Form 10-K, quarterly reports on Form 10-Q, and current reports on Form 8-K.

You should note that lawyers use the terms "reporting company," "public company," and "publicly-traded company" interchangeably. They all mean the same thing.

B. What Companies Are Required to File Periodic Reports?

If a company gets large enough, the federal securities laws require it to file periodic reports with the SEC. There are three types of reporting companies:

Section 12(b). Companies with a class of securities—either stock or debt—trading on a national securities exchange are required by the '34 Act to register with the SEC. *See* Securities Exchange Act of 1934 § 12(b). You're probably familiar with the two largest national securities exchanges: the New York Stock Exchange (NYSE) and the Nasdaq Stock Market (NASDAQ). Registration under Section 12 triggers the '34 Act's periodic reporting requirement. *See* Securities Exchange Act of 1934 § 13(a).

Section 12(g)(1). But what if the company's securities don't trade on a national securities exchange? After all, many companies don't qualify to have their securities listed on a national securities exchange. In this case, securities are often traded through private sales between two parties in so-called "over-the-counter" transactions. Whether these companies have to file periodic reports with the SEC depends on how many shareholders they have.

Specifically, under Section 12(g)(1), these companies will have to register with the SEC if they have:

- More than $10 million in assets; *and*
- A class of equity securities held of record by *either*:
  - 2,000 persons, or
  - 500 persons who are not "accredited investors"[1]

---

[1] Yes, this is the same definition of "accredited investor" that's used in the Regulation D exemption discussed in Chapter 5.

You may think that the numerical requirements seem low. After all, public companies typically have hundreds of thousands, if not millions, of shareholders. But note that the statute refers to shareholders *"of record."* A shareholder of record refers to the shareholder whose name appears in the company's records as owning the securities. However, the names of most shareholders of public companies don't appear on the company's records. The record owners are broker-dealers, banks, or depositaries that hold the securities on behalf of the true "beneficial" shareholder. This means that one shareholder of record may hold securities for thousands of beneficial owners. Thus, 2,000 shareholders of record represent a LOT of shareholders—and certainly enough to create a public trading market for the company's securities.

Once again, the company's registration under Section 12 triggers the '34 Act's periodic reporting requirements. *See* Securities Exchange Act of 1934 § 13(a).

Section 15(d). The final type of public company is a corporation that has gone public by selling securities through an effective registration statement but for whatever reason doesn't fall within either Section 12(b) or Section 12(g)(1). These companies won't be required to register with the SEC, but they nonetheless will have to file periodic reports with the SEC because they chose to sell securities to the public. *See* Securities Exchange Act of 1934 § 15(d).

C. Periodic Reports

Each year, public companies are required to file annual, quarterly, and episodic "current" reports with the SEC. These reports take over where the Registration Statement ends. Periodic reports are intended to give the public all the information needed to make investment decisions about the company.

1. Form 10-K: The Annual Report

The Form 10-K must be filed once a year with the SEC. It sets forth a comprehensive picture of the public company, including such information as:

- The company's business
- The risks associated with investing in the company
- The company's properties
- The company's legal proceedings
- The trading market for the company's common stock
- The company's board of directors
- The company's senior management
- The company's major stockholders
- Executive compensation
- Several years of financial statements, including balance sheets and income statements, that have been audited by an independent accounting firm
- Management's discussion and analysis of its financial condition (the MD&A)
- Information about the effectiveness of the company's internal controls
- Copies of the company's organizational documents and important contracts

The filing due date depends on how well established the company is. "Large accelerated filers" have 60 days following the end of their fiscal year to file the 10-K. "Accelerated files" have 75 days. All other companies have 90 days.

A "large accelerated filer" must have a public float of at least $700 million. In addition, it must have been a reporting company for at least 12 months and must have filed at least one Form 10-K. If this definition seems familiar to you, it's probably because it's similar to the definition of well-known seasoned issuer (WKSI) found in the '33 Act.

An "accelerated filer" must have a public float between $75 million and $700 million. In addition, it must have been a reporting company for at least 12 months and must have filed at least one Form 10-K. Once again, if this definition seems familiar to you, it's probably because it's similar to the definition of seasoned issuer found in the '33 Act.

2. *Form 10-Q: The Quarterly Report*

The Form 10-Q must be filed for the first three quarters in each fiscal year; the Form 10-K replaces what would have been the fourth quarter Form 10-Q. The Form 10-Q isn't nearly as exhaustive as the Form 10-K. It doesn't require the company to disclose all of the same categories of information appearing in the Form 10-K. Instead, the Form 10-Q basically consists of quarterly financial statements (which are unaudited) and information related to the quarterly financial statements, such as the MD&A and the company's evaluation of its internal controls. In general, the only information from the Form 10-K that must be updated in the Form 10-Q is disclosure about the risk factors associated with investing in the company.

Large accelerated filers and accelerated filers have 40 days from the end of the fiscal quarter to file their Form 10-Q with the SEC, while all other filers have 45 days.

3. *Form 8-K: The Current Report*

Rather than being triggered by the passage of time, the Form 8-K is triggered by the occurrence of a specific event set forth in the Form 8-K. The idea underlying the Form 8-K is that some information is so important to investors that it can't wait until the next Form 10-Q or Form 10-K to be disclosed. To protect investors, the information needs to be disclosed now—or, to be precise, within four business days of the event.

Not surprisingly, many of the triggers reflect extremely important events, such as:

- The company filing for bankruptcy
- The delisting of a company's stock
- The company changing its independent accounting firm
- The hiring or departure of a company's senior officer
- The appointment or departure of a member of the board of directors
- The amendment of the company's certificate of incorporation or bylaws

But the triggering events have expanded over the last few years, and so they also include more run of the mill events, such as:

- The company entering into an important contract
- The company becoming subject to a direct financial obligation or off-balance sheet obligation
- The company announcing its quarterly or annual financial results
- The company experiencing a cybersecurity incident

Thus, nowadays, public companies have to disclose much more information to the public under Form 8-K.

D. Disclosures to Avoid Making a Misleading Statement

Finally, the federal securities laws require public companies to be completely accurate whenever they disclose information in their periodic reports. No half-truths. This means that public companies might have to disclose additional information to make sure their statements don't mislead investors.

Specifically, Rule 12b-20 provides that when a public company discloses information in response to the line items provided in a Form 10-K, Form 10-Q, Form 8-K, or Proxy Statement, it must also disclose "such further material information, if any, as may be necessary to make the required statements . . . not misleading." Let's see how this works.

Assume that a sneaker company spent a significant amount of money to upgrade its inventory control system. It completed the upgrade, but, unfortunately, it was having a lot of problems implementing it. In its Form 10-K, the company stated that: "We have rolled out a new and updated Inventory Management System (IMS), enabling us to nearly double the number of products available for sale online by exposing inventory in all our stores as well as throughout our supply chain." On its face, this was a true statement. The company *did* roll out a new and updated inventory control system. And the inventory control system *did* double the number of products available online. That sounds like good news to investors. But the company left out the bad news—that the inventory control system wasn't working well. The company's statement was misleading. Rule 12b-20 would require the company to disclose in the Form 10-K the problems the company was experiencing in rolling out the new system.

E. Quick Recap

Investor protection doesn't just stop when a company sells securities to the public. Obviously, shareholders of public companies need information, too. Investors need to decide whether to buy or sell a company's stock in the aftermarket, and they need information to make these decisions. That's why the '34 Act requires certain companies to file reports with the SEC on a periodic basis. These companies are referred to as "reporting" or "public" companies. While the '34 Act includes three definitions of reporting companies that you need to know, the definitions essentially boil down to companies that have publicly-traded securities.

Reporting companies are required to file a Form 10-K at the end of each year and a Form 10-Q at the end of the first three quarters of the fiscal year. A Form 8-K must be filed following the occurrence of specific triggering events. In the past, the Form 8-K was only required for very significant events, but that's changed. Nowadays, be aware that there are many more triggers that require public companies to disclose information in the Form 8-K, which is bringing the '34 Act's periodic reporting regime closer to a continuous reporting regime.

CHAPTER 9

Proxy Regulation

A. Introduction

The '34 Act regulates proxy voting at public companies. Not surprisingly, the primary goal of the proxy rules is to ensure that shareholders have enough information to make informed voting decisions. But there's another goal: improving shareholder democracy. In other words, the SEC has recognized the collective action problems inherent in public companies and has tried to find ways to improve the voting process to make directors more accountable to shareholders. Therefore, several proxy rules are intended to encourage shareholders to participate more fully in director elections.

B. Routine Shareholder Meetings

Every year, corporations are required to hold an annual shareholders' meeting for the election of directors. Public companies have so many shareholders that voting must occur by proxy. This means that shareholders vote without being physically present at the meeting. So each year, public companies send "proxy cards"—which are similar to ballots—to their shareholders.

Shareholders vote by completing and returning the proxy cards. Nowadays, shareholders can also vote by telephone or through the Internet.

Not surprisingly, the '34 Act requires public companies[1] to provide a disclosure document to their shareholders so that they can make informed voting decisions. Specifically, Rule 14a-3 provides that no one can "solicit" proxies from a public company's shareholders unless the shareholders are provided with a "Proxy Statement." This is the heart of the '34 Act's proxy rules.

The Proxy Statement contains information about the meeting: when it is, where it is, how to vote, etc. It also includes information about the items up for shareholder vote. For example, when directors are being elected, the Proxy Statement includes extensive information about each nominee's background. It also provides general information about the board, such as board leadership, board structure, board responsibilities, and board committees.

Interestingly, the Proxy Statement doesn't disclose information about the company's operations or financial performance—although most shareholders would presumably want that information before they cast their votes for directors. The shareholders will get that information in a second document: the Annual Report to Securityholders (ARS). *See* Securities Exchange Act of 1934 Rule 14a-3(b). While some public companies prepare an ARS for their shareholders, the SEC permits public companies to use the company's Form 10-K as its ARS, and many public companies choose to do that.

The company can meet the delivery requirements by either (1) posting the proxy materials on the company's website and then

---

[1] While all public companies are required to file periodic reports with the SEC, only Section 12 companies are subject to the proxy rules. In other words, the proxy rules don't apply to companies that are required to file periodic reports with the SEC because of Section 15(d).

mailing a "Notice of Internet Availability" to each shareholder; or (2) mailing the proxy materials to each shareholder. The company must also file its proxy materials with the SEC on first use. *See* Securities Exchange Act of 1934 Rule 14a-16.

Annual meetings typically occur five or six months after the end of the company's fiscal year. That means that "proxy season" for companies with a fiscal year ending December 31st is late April through early June.

C. When It's Not So Routine

For routine elections of directors, the proxy rules are pretty straightforward: the company sends out proxy cards to its shareholders, which triggers its filing and delivery obligations under the proxy rules. However, sometimes circumstances aren't so routine. Sometimes shareholders aren't happy with the company's policies, and they want to send a message to the board. Sometimes shareholders aren't happy with the company's board, and they want to talk to each other about options. Sometimes shareholders want to nominate individuals to serve on the board or even engage in a proxy fight. How do the proxy rules work in these situations?

1. Shareholder Proposals

Sometimes, shareholders want to ask the company's management to make changes to its operations or its governance structure. Typically, this is through Rule 14a-8. Rule 14a-8 requires a public company to include a shareholder proposal submitted by a qualified shareholder on the company's proxy card and in the company's proxy statement—even if the board doesn't want to include it. This gives the company's shareholders the opportunity to vote on the proposal.

First things first. What's a "shareholder proposal?" When shareholders are asked to vote, the vote is done through a *proposal*. At public companies, it's usually the corporation's management that makes a proposal. For example, at each annual shareholders' meeting, company management will make a proposal recommending that shareholders should vote for each of the company's board nominees. That's an example of a management proposal. When shareholders make the request, the proposals are called *shareholder proposals*.

Most shareholder proposals are made by activist investors who use the shareholder process to encourage the company to make changes to its policies or its behavior. Some shareholder proposals attempt to improve the company's corporate governance practices. For example, a shareholder proposal might recommend that the company separate the CEO and Board Chair positions. Other kinds of shareholder proposals attempt to make the company more socially responsible. For example, a shareholder proposal might recommend that the company prepare a report on the company's carbon emissions.

Why did the SEC decide to adopt Rule 14a-8? In short, the SEC wanted to encourage shareholders to communicate with each other and with company management about important corporate policies. Without Rule 14a-8, shareholders would be unlikely to submit matters for shareholder vote. That's because the proxy rules require *anyone* soliciting proxies to provide shareholders with a proxy statement so that they can make informed voting decisions. *See* Securities Exchange Act of 1934 Rule 14a-3(a). So, for example, without Rule 14a-8, a shareholder that wanted shareholders to vote on a proposal asking the board to reduce the company's carbon emissions would have to prepare and deliver its own proxy statement to the company's shareholders. That would be prohibitively expensive. With Rule 14a-8, the shareholder proposal would appear on the company's proxy statement, free of charge to the shareholder.

Notice that Rule 14a-8 is a substantive, not disclosure rule; it regulates the conduct of public companies. Rule 14a-8 requires public companies to take certain action—*i.e.*, to include shareholder proposals in the company's proxy materials. We know that most SEC rules are disclosure driven, so Rule 14a-8 is something different.

If the shareholder proposal is approved by the shareholders, is the board required to do what the proposal says? In general, no. As discussed below, that's because most shareholder proposals are written as requests, recommendations, or suggestions. Therefore, the board is free to ignore most successful shareholder proposals.

There are a few situations when the company can omit the shareholder proposal from the company's proxy materials. Rule 14a-8(i) sets forth 13 exclusions which allow the company to omit the shareholder proposal from the company's proxy materials. Your professor will probably focus on two of them: the "improper under state law" exclusion and the "management functions" exclusion. So those are the ones we'll focus on, too.

Improper Under State Law. Rule 14a-8(i)(1) allows the company to omit the shareholder proposal from its proxy materials if "the proposal is not a proper subject for action by shareholders under the laws of the jurisdiction of the company's organization." The exclusion makes sense because without it, the company would be required to do something that shareholders aren't permitted to require under state corporate law.

As you might remember from your Business Organizations course, state corporate law statutes—such as Section 141 of the Delaware General Corporation Law—distribute power to boards and shareholders. The board of directors, not shareholders, makes business decisions. The power of shareholders is generally limited to electing the directors. A shareholder proposal purporting to take management rights away from management or to give management rights to shareholders would be "improper under state law." The "improper under state law" exclusion recognizes that companies shouldn't be forced to include illegal proposals in their proxy materials.

A shareholder proposal that requests, recommends, or urges the board to make a particular decision or take a particular action isn't improper under state law because the board doesn't have to obey it. This is why so many shareholder proposals are drafted as recommendations. These "precatory" proposals can't be excluded as improper under state law under Rule 14a-8(i)(1).

On the other hand, a shareholder proposal that would be binding on the board might be improper under state law. What would bind a board? The company's bylaws! This means that shareholder proposals asking the shareholders to amend the company's bylaws might be excludable as improper under state law. It depends on the substance of the bylaw. If the bylaw relates to business decisions, then it's excludable—because shareholders don't get to tell the board how to manage the company. But if the bylaw relates to voting rights, then it won't be excludable—because shareholders are empowered under corporate law to vote.

So, for example, a shareholder proposal asking shareholders to approve a bylaw amendment that would require a majority vote, rather than a plurality vote, to elect directors would not be improper under state law. Although binding on the board, it relates to voting, which is what shareholders do under state corporate law. On the other hand, a shareholder proposal asking shareholders to approve a bylaw amendment that would forbid a company from doing business in a particular country without shareholder approval would be improper under state law. The substance of the bylaw relates to the business of the company, and state law gives that authority to the board, not the shareholders. Therefore, the company could exclude this shareholder proposal.

Management Functions. Even if the shareholder proposal is written as a recommendation, it can be excluded if it "deals with a matter relating to the company's ordinary business operations." *See* Securities Exchange Act of 1934 Rule 14a-8(i)(7). This exclusion recognizes that company management is supposed to handle the company's day-to-day operations, not the shareholders.

However, if the shareholder proposal addresses a significant social issue that "transcends" the company's day-to-day operations, it can't be excluded. The idea is that shareholders should be able to vote on proposals that raise significant policy concerns. The "transcendence" exception is why so many socially significant shareholder proposals have appeared in company proxy materials. For example, a shareholder proposal that requests the board of directors to prepare a public report evaluating the effectiveness of the company's efforts to prevent employment discrimination would not be excludable under Rule 14a-8(i)(7). Even though the company's employment decisions and practices are classic examples of ordinary business operations, employment discrimination is a matter of social significance that transcends the company's day-to-day operations.

In applying the "transcendence" exception, the SEC has struggled with whether or not the significant social issue must have a connection to the company. In other words, what if the shareholder proposal relates to an issue that's significant to society in general, but doesn't have much to do with the specific company? If the transcendence exception applies in this situation, critics argue that Rule 14a-8 will be turned into a tool of social activism and not shareholder democracy. Currently, the SEC has determined that the transcendence exception requires a company-specific analysis, meaning that the policy issue raised by the shareholder proposal must be significant to the company. If it's not, the shareholder proposal can be excluded because it "deals with a matter relating to the company's ordinary business operations." *See* Securities Exchange Act of 1934 Rule 14a-8(i)(7).

2. Shareholder Communications

When shareholders are unhappy, they may want to talk to each other about the upcoming board election. However, because these communications would be "solicitations" under Rule 14a-1(*l*), the unhappy shareholders would have to comply with the filing and delivery requirements of the proxy rules. This would obviously chill communication between and among shareholders, which is not a good thing for shareholder democracy. Therefore, the SEC adopted several rules to address this problem and encourage shareholder communications.

First, shareholders don't have to worry about the filing and delivery requirements of the proxy rules if they're simply communicating to influence the outcome of the election (and not seeking proxies). *See* Securities Exchange Act of 1934 Rule 14a-2(b). This rule permits shareholders to engage in so-called "withhold the vote" campaigns, which encourage shareholders to send a message to the company by voting "no" on one or more of the company's nominees.

Second, the proxy rules allow shareholders to solicit up to ten persons without triggering the filing and delivery requirements of the proxy rules. *See* Securities Exchange Act of 1934 Rule 14a-2(b).

Third, shareholders who aren't seeking proxies are free to make public statements—such as through press releases, social media, or newspaper ads—of how they intend to vote. *See* Securities Exchange Act of 1934 Rule 14a-1(*l*)(2)(iv). This rule is primarily used by influential shareholders who are hoping to influence the results of a shareholder vote.

Finally, even shareholders who do plan to seek proxies can communicate with fellow shareholders without filing or delivering a proxy statement so long as they deliver the proxy statement before or at the same time a form of proxy card is provided to the shareholders. *See* Securities Exchange Act of 1934 Rule 14a-12. This rule includes several other conditions, including the requirement that all written materials must be filed with the SEC on the date of first use. Rule 14a-12 is a real game changer because it allows solicitations to be made before a proxy statement is filed with the SEC and disseminated to shareholders.

3. *Proxy Access*

Sometimes shareholders want to do more than talk. These shareholders want action. Specifically, they may want to nominate their own individuals to serve on the company's board. This will give shareholders a choice when they vote. The problem is that nominating directors triggers the proxy rules, meaning that the shareholder would have to file a proxy statement with the SEC and deliver proxy statements to the company's shareholders. These costs tend to discourage shareholders from nominating directors.

Note that the shareholder proposal rule of Rule 14a-8 can't be used by shareholders to nominate directors. There's an exclusion for shareholder proposals that "seek[ ] to include a specific individual in the company's proxy materials for election to the board of directors. *See* Securities Exchange Act of 1934 Rule 14a-8(i)(8).

In 2010, the SEC tried to change this. Hoping to improve corporate democracy, the SEC adopted a rule that would've required public companies to include shareholder nominees in the company's proxy materials at company expense. However, the rule was struck down by the DC Circuit. *See* Business Roundtable v. SEC, 647 F.3d 1144 (D.C. Cir. 2011).

Rather than re-proposing the rule, the SEC urged companies to adopt bylaws that would require them to include shareholder nominated directors in the company's proxy materials. In response, many public companies have adopted "proxy access bylaws." Typically, proxy access bylaws allow qualified shareholders to nominate two or three directors for election to the board. For example, assuming that a company's board consists of 11 directors, there could be 14 nominees on the company's proxy card—11 individuals nominated by the company and three individuals nominated by the qualified shareholder. Proxy access bylaws don't allow shareholders to get control over the company's board, but they do give shareholders a choice in director elections. They also provide activist shareholders with an opportunity to obtain representation on the company's board.

4. Proxy Fights

If a shareholder wants to obtain control over the board of directors, the shareholder must engage in a proxy fight by filing its own proxy materials with the SEC and delivering its own proxy materials to company shareholders.

In a proxy fight, both the shareholder and company management will no doubt be doing a lot of smack talking, through letters to shareholders, through press releases, and through social media and website postings. Each side will try to persuade company shareholders to vote for its slate of directors. Ordinarily, these communications would be considered "solicitations," triggering the filing and delivery requirements of the proxy rules. However, the shareholder and the company can make these communications before furnishing a proxy statement as long as Rule 14a-12 is met.

In a proxy fight, the public company and the insurgent shareholder are required to use a "universal proxy card" to solicit proxies. *See* Securities Exchange Act of 1934 Rule 14a-19. A universal proxy card lists all nominees—from the shareholder and from the company—on one card. So, for example, in a contested election for 12 open board positions, there could be as many as 24 nominees. The proxy card will have 24 names on it, permitting the shareholders to pick and choose between all of the nominees.

5. Quick Recap

Whenever anyone asks a shareholder of a public company for his vote, the proxy rules kick in. To promote informed voting decisions, the soliciting person must provide the shareholders with a Proxy Statement and file the Proxy Statement with the SEC.

The SEC has identified a second goal of the proxy rules: to encourage shareholder participation in the voting process. For example, to encourage shareholders to talk with each other about director elections, the SEC eliminated the delivery and filing requirements for many shareholder solicitations. In addition, the SEC adopted Rule 14a-8, which requires public companies to include proposals made by shareholders in the company's proxy materials, unless an exclusion is available.

CHAPTER 10

Mergers and Acquisitions

A. Introduction

As you might remember from your Business Organizations class, there are two primary M&A structures used by public companies: the merger and the stock acquisition/tender offer. M&A transactions are certainly governed by state corporate law, but when public companies are involved, the federal securities laws may be triggered as well.

B. Mergers

First, the proxy rules will be implicated if shareholders are required to approve the merger. State corporate law typically requires the shareholders of the target company to approve a merger. If the target corporation is a public company, it will have to solicit proxies from its shareholders—which in turn will trigger the proxy rules. That means that the target company will have to file a proxy statement with the SEC and furnish its proxy statement to its shareholders.

The proxy statement will contain information needed by shareholders to help them make an informed decision about whether to approve the merger, including a summary of the terms of the merger and copies of any fairness opinion obtained by the target company's board of directors.

C. Tender Offers

A tender offer is a type of stock purchase. In a tender offer, a bidder makes a public offer to purchase the stock of a target company. The '34 Act includes several specialized rules regulating tender offers for public companies.[1] They were a response to the abusive tender offer practices that were typical in the late 1960s. At that time, hostile tender offers were often launched on a Friday or Saturday night with little information and short deadlines, the so-called "Saturday Night Special." This combination coerced target shareholders into making rushed and uninformed decision on whether to sell their stock to the bidder. Congress responded through the Williams Act, which amended the '34 Act to require bidders to provide information when launching a tender offer for the common stock of a public company. However, Congress didn't stop there. It also imposed substantive rules that regulate the public company tender offer process.

1. Section 13(d)

Section 13(d) requires anyone who acquires more than 5% of the common stock of a public company to disclose their stock ownership by filing a Schedule 13D with the SEC within five business days of crossing the 5% threshold. *See* Securities Exchange Act of 1934 Rule 13d-1. What's the purpose of this filing? At least one

---

[1] Like the proxy rules, the tender offer rules apply only to Section 12 public companies. In other words, a public company that files periodic reports under Section 15(d) doesn't have to comply with the '34 Act's tender offer rules.

purpose is to give the target company a "heads up" that a tender offer is on its way. That's because the Schedule 13D requires the purchaser to disclose, among other things, the purpose of the acquisition and any takeover plans.

While Section 13(d) is implicated in most tender offers, note that it applies whenever the 5% ownership threshold is crossed, even when the acquiring company isn't planning to launch a tender offer.

2. Tender Offer Disclosure

The '34 Act requires the bidder to provide disclosure to the target's shareholders so that they can make informed decisions about whether to sell their stock in the tender offer. *See* Securities Exchange Act of 1934 Section 14(d). The bidder must file a Schedule TO with the SEC on the date of commencement of the tender offer.

In addition, the bidder must disseminate its tender offer materials—including the written "Offer To Purchase"—to the target company's shareholders. This is typically done through a "summary publication:" a page-long "tombstone" advertisement placed in national newspapers that announces the tender offer and sets forth the basic terms of the tender offer, including the number of shares to be purchased, the purchase price, and the deadline to tender. The bidder then follows up by mailing its tender offer materials to the target company's shareholders. *See* Securities Exchange Act of 1934 Rule 14d-4 and Rule 14d-6.

The '34 Act also requires the target company to provide information to its shareholders. Specifically, within ten business days of the start of the tender offer, the target is required to take a public position on the tender offer. In other words, the securities laws don't allow the target company to remain silent. It must disclose whether it recommends accepting (or rejecting) the tender offer or whether it's remaining neutral. *See* Securities Exchange Act of 1934 Rule 14e-2.

The target company's public statement then triggers another disclosure requirement. On the date it makes its public statement, the target must file a Schedule 14D-9 with the SEC. *See* Securities Exchange Act of 1934 Rule 14d-9. The Schedule 14D-9 sets forth the target company's recommendation, as well as an explanation for its recommendation. In other words, if the target company has recommended that its shareholders shouldn't tender, it will have to explain the reasons for this recommendation and provide support for its recommendation, such as a fairness opinion showing that the bidder's offer is too low.

3. *Tender Offer "Rules of the Road"*

The tender offer rules also impose substantive rules on how the tender offer must be conducted. Specifically, there are seven "rules of the road" that are intended to eliminate the coercive practices of the Saturday Night Special:

- Minimum Duration Rule: the tender offer must be kept open for at least 20 business days. *See* Securities Exchange Act of 1934 Rule 14e-1(a).
- Withdrawal Rights Rule: target shareholders who tendered their stock must be permitted to change their mind and get their stock back during the entire duration of the tender offer. *See* Securities Exchange Act of 1934 Section 14(d)(5) and Rule 14d-7.
- Highest Consideration Rule: if the bidder increases the tender offer price, it must pay all shareholders, regardless of when they tendered, the highest tender offer price that was offered. *See* Securities Exchange Act of 1934 Section 14(d)(7).
- Pro-ration Rule: in an oversubscribed tender offer—where more shares were tendered than the bidder

offered to purchase—the bidder must purchase the tendered stock on a pro-rated basis, as opposed to on a first come, first served basis. *See* Securities Exchange Act of 1934 Section 14(d)(6) and Rule 14d-8.

- Prompt Payment or Return Rule: the bidder must promptly pay for the stock or, if the tender offer wasn't successful, it must promptly return all tendered stock to the shareholders. *See* Securities Exchange Act of 1934 Rule 14e-1(c).
- All Holders Rule: the tender offer must be open to all shareholders—including the bidder. *See* Securities Exchange Act of 1934 Rule 14d-10(a)(1).
- Best Price Rule: all shareholders must receive the same tender offer consideration; *i.e.*, the bidder can't make side deals to certain shareholders to encourage them to participate in the tender offer. *See* Rule 14d-10(a)(2).

D. Securities Issued in M&A Transactions

In M&A transactions, the acquiring corporation often uses its own securities as a form of consideration, rather than cash, to buy the target company. For example, in a stock-for-stock merger, the acquiring company might offer two shares of its stock for each share of the target company's stock. It works the same way in tender offers. The acquiring company may offer to pay the target company shareholders with shares of the acquiring company's stock. In these cases, the acquiring company is offering to sell securities to the target shareholders. Even though the acquiring company isn't receiving cash for the sales, Section 5 of the '33 Act is still implicated. In general, that means that the offering must be registered with the SEC.

The '33 Act provides a specialized form of registration statement to be used in M&A transactions: the Registration Statement on Form S-4. The Form S-4 includes information about the acquiring company, the target company, and the M&A transaction. In addition, if the M&A transaction requires a shareholder vote, the Form S-4 can also be used as a proxy statement. For example, the SEC permits the parties to a merger to combine the target company's proxy statement with the acquiring company's registration statement in the Form S-4. The Form S-4 operates as both a registration statement under the '33 Act and a proxy statement under the '34 Act.

The '34 Act also includes special gun jumping rules that apply to "business combination transactions" that make it much easier for the companies to communicate about the M&A transaction without violating Section 5. *See* Securities Act of 1933 Rule 165. You might remember from Chapter 4 that offers can't be made during the pre-filing period. But the SEC recognized that companies using stock to acquire another company needed to communicate with shareholders before a registration statement was filed with the SEC. Therefore, the SEC promulgated Rule 165, which allows offers during the pre-filing period, as long as written offers include a legend (urging shareholders to read the registration statement when it's available) and are filed with the SEC on the date of first use.

Finally, if the target company isn't public, the acquiring company may be able to rely on an exemption from Section 5, such as Regulation D, to issue the securities without registration. However, if the target company is a public company, no exemption will be available.

E. Going Private

When a public company is acquired, it often becomes a private company—meaning that it will no longer be required to file periodic reports, comply with the proxy rules, or comply with the tender offer rules. When does a company go private? It depends on how the company became a public company in the first place:

Source of Reporting Obligations	Company Became a Public Company Because:	Reporting Obligations Are Terminated When:
Section 12(b)	Company has a class of security that's listed on a national securities exchange	The class of security has been de-listed from the national securities exchange
Section 12(g)(1)	Company has more than $10 million in assets and a class of equity securities held of record by either • 2,000 persons; or • 500 non-accredited investors	The class of security is: • held by fewer than 300 shareholders of record; or • held by fewer than 500 shareholders of record, where the total assets of the issuer have not exceeded $10 million for last three years

Section 15(d)	Company has a class of security that was sold in an offering registered under the '33 Act	The class of security is: • held by fewer than 300 shareholders of record; or • held by fewer than 500 shareholders of record, where the total assets of the issuer have not exceeded $10 million for last three years

When a company goes private, it must a file a Schedule 13E-3 with the SEC and furnish similar information to its shareholders. Among other things, the target must discuss the purpose of the transaction and state whether the company believes the transaction is fair to the company's shareholders. *See* Securities Exchange Act of 1934 Rule 13e-3. These additional disclosures reflect the SEC's concern that going private transactions can treat public shareholders badly. After all, companies typically go public at high stock prices and often go private when the company's stock is trading at historically low prices.

F. Quick Recap

When an M&A transaction involves a public company, the federal securities laws are implicated. Not surprisingly, the '34 Act requires mandatory disclosure so that the shareholders of the target company can make informed decisions about whether to approve a merger or to sell their stock in a tender offer. More surprisingly, in addition to disclosure rules, the SEC adopted substantive rules that regulate how tender offers can be conducted. These rules of the road are intended to reduce the coercive nature of tender offers and give the target shareholders enough time to process the information they've been given.

CHAPTER 11

Securities Fraud

A. Introduction

As we know, the federal securities laws are about investor protection. Requiring disclosure is an important part of investor protection but so is preventing fraud. The primary anti-fraud provision is Rule 10b-5, which states that:

> It shall be unlawful for any person, directly or indirectly, by the use of any means or instrumentality of interstate commerce, or of the mails or of any facility of any national securities exchange,
>
> (a) To employ any device, scheme, or artifice to defraud,
>
> (b) To make any untrue statement of a material fact or to omit to state a material fact necessary in order to make the statements made, in the light of the circumstances under which they were made, not misleading, or

> (c) To engage in any act, practice, or course of business which operates or would operate as a fraud or deceit upon any person,
>
> in connection with the purchase or sale of any security.

Rule 10b-5 reaches all types of securities fraud, but in this chapter we're going to focus on the most litigated type of securities fraud: claims that a public company made false or misleading statements to the investing public. These are often referred to as "fraud-on-the-market" cases.

B. Rule 10b-5 and the Private Securities Fraud Class Action

Rule 10b-5 doesn't expressly authorize investors to sue for securities fraud; the rule simply says that "it shall be unlawful" to commit securities fraud. You might think that this means that only the SEC can sue to enforce Rule 10b-5, but a long time ago the courts determined that Congress meant to allow investors to sue wrongdoers for securities fraud, too. In other words, the courts *implied* a private right of action under Rule 10b-5.

Fraud-on-the-market claims are often brought as class actions. That's because in a typical fraud-on-the-market case, it doesn't make economic sense for most investors to bring individual claims against the company. Their damages are just too small to justify hiring a lawyer. In a class action, an investor acts as a representative for the class, filing an action on behalf of the entire class of investors who suffered losses.

If the plaintiff is claiming that the company made false or misleading statements that artificially inflated the company's stock price, the class will include all investors who purchased stock between the date the misstatement was made and the date the fraud was revealed to the public. This period of time between the day the false or misleading statement was made and the day the fraud was revealed to the public is referred to as the "class period."

Class actions are governed by Rule 23 of the Federal Rules of Civil Procedure, which requires the federal court to certify the action as a class action. In making its determination, the court will consider (1) whether the size of the class is too large for the FRCP's joinder rules to work; (2) whether the claim implicates common questions of law and fact; (3) whether the representative's claims are typical of the class claims; and (4) whether the representative is able to protect the interests of the class. *See* FRCP Rule 23(a). If the court finds that these four pre-requisites are satisfied, it can certify the class action if "questions of law or fact common to class members predominate over questions affecting only individual members" and the court determines that the class action is the best way to proceed. *See* FRCP Rule 23(b)(3).

C. Elements of a Fraud-on-the-Market Claim

Remember that Rule 10b-5 has three subsections. To determine the necessary elements of the claim, we have to determine which subsection of Rule 10b-5 has been violated. In fraud-on-the-market actions, the underlying claim is that the public company lied to investors, *i.e.*, that the company made a false or misleading statement. Therefore, fraud-on-the-market claims fall within subsection (b) of Rule 10b-5.

The elements of a fraud-on-the-market claim are:

1. False or Misleading Statement

Under Rule 10b-5, a statement is fraudulent if it is either false or misleading. Falsity is easy to understand: it's an affirmatively inaccurate statement. A good example would be a public company's Income Statement that overstates the company's revenue or a company's statement denying that it's engaged in merger negotiations when it really is.

The concept of a misleading statement may be a little more difficult to understand. Rule 10b-5 states that it's unlawful to "omit to state a material fact necessary in order to make the statements made, in the light of the circumstances under which they were made, not misleading." In other words, the company said something that might be technically true, but it left out part of the story—usually some bad news. A misleading statement is a half-truth. You might remember that we introduced this concept in Chapter 8.

Let's use a similar hypothetical. Assume that a sneaker company spent a significant amount of money to upgrade its inventory control system. It completed the upgrade, but, unfortunately, it was having a lot of problems implementing it. In a press release, the company stated that: "We have rolled out a new and updated Inventory Control System (ICS), enabling us to nearly double the number of products available for sale online by exposing inventory in all our stores as well as throughout our supply chain." On its face, this was a true statement. The company *did* roll out a new and updated inventory control system. And the inventory control system *did* double the number of products available online. That sounds like good news to investors. But the company left out the bad news—that the inventory control system wasn't working well. The company's statement was misleading, and the company runs the risk of being sued for securities fraud under Rule 10b-5.

On the other hand, what if the sneaker company issued an earnings forecast, but didn't say anything about its inventory control system? Did the failure to disclose the problems with the inventory control system make the statement made (the earnings forecast) misleading? Probably not. That's because courts don't want to turn Rule 10b-5—a fraud rule—into a de facto disclosure rule that requires a company to disclose all negative information whenever it speaks. For the statement to be fraudulent, there must be a close connection between the omitted information and the company's statement.

So when you're determining whether a statement is misleading, you should think about the following three things:

- Did the company make a statement?
- Did the company omit information from that statement?
- How close was the connection between the omitted information and the statement that was made?

The closer the connection, the more likely it is that the company's statement would be considered misleading under Rule 10b-5.

2. *Of Material Fact*

Not all false or misleading statements are violations of Rule 10b-5. They must be false or misleading statements of *material* fact. As introduced in Chapter 1, information is material if there's a substantial likelihood that a reasonable investor would find the information important in deciding how to act. *See* TSC Industries, Inc. v. Northway, Inc., 426 U.S. 438 (1976). This definition should always be the starting point of a materiality analysis.

Materiality is an extremely fact specific inquiry. But there are a few things to keep in mind. First, there's a low threshold for materiality. To be material, the information must be significant to investors, but it doesn't need to be so important that it would cause investors to change their minds. That said, statements that are extremely vague or excessively optimistic—such as the company is doing "fine" or a new product will be a "gamechanger"—won't meet the threshold. That's because reasonable investors are presumed to understand that "puffery" is promotional sales talk.

Second, the materiality analysis is contextual. In other words, in determining whether information is material, courts will put it in context by considering the surrounding circumstances, including other information that's available. In *TSC Industries*, the Supreme Court recognized the contextual nature of materiality when it restated the materiality test described above as "[p]ut another way, there must be a substantial likelihood that the disclosure of the omitted fact would have been viewed by the reasonable investor as having significantly altered the 'total mix' of information made available." *See id.*

We also see the contextual nature of materiality in the "truth on the market" defense and the "bespeaks caution doctrine."

Defendants in fraud-on-the-market actions commonly argue that the company's statement isn't material because the market was already aware of the true state of affairs. Under this "truth on the market" defense, the court won't just look at the company's statement in isolation. In determining materiality, the court will consider other information that's known to the market. For example, the Supreme Court recognized that "publishing accurate facts in a proxy statement can render a misleading proposition too unimportant to ground liability." *See* Virginia Bankshares, Inc. v. Sandberg, 501 U.S. 1083, 1097 (1991).

Similarly, when a court is asked to determine the materiality of forward-looking statements—such as projections, forecasts, and statements of plans or objectives—the court will also consider any cautionary statements made by the company. According to the bespeaks caution doctrine, "[c]autionary language, if sufficient, renders the alleged omissions or misrepresentations immaterial as a matter of law." *See In re* Donald J. Trump Casino Securities Litig., 7 F.3d 357 (3d Cir. 1993).

The challenge with the bespeaks caution doctrine is determining whether the cautionary statements are sufficient.

Boilerplate warnings—such as general cautions about possible "changes in economic conditions" or "reduced customer demand"—won't meet the threshold in most jurisdictions. The best cautionary statements are those that are tailored to the risk of the forward-looking statement and those that are specific to the company and its operations.

Finally, there is a special materiality test used for "speculative information." Speculative information refers to events that may or may not occur. Think of two companies that are negotiating a merger. Are these merger negotiations material? Shareholders of the target company would probably think so because if the merger goes through, they'll be paid a significant premium for their stock. But what if the merger negotiations just started? At this point, it's just as likely that the merger will fail to go through, and, if so, the target's shareholders won't get a premium. Thus, the materiality of the merger negotiations turns on how likely it is that the merger will occur.

The Supreme Court recognized this and adopted a balancing test for determining the materiality of speculative information. *See* Basic v. Levinson, 485 U.S. 224 (1988). Under this test, the probability of the event occurring will be balanced against the magnitude of the event. This means that a very important event with a very low probability of occurring might nonetheless constitute material information.

3. In Connection with the Purchase or Sale of a Security

The "in connection with" element turns a fraud claim into a securities fraud claim. Note that in a fraud-on-the-market action, the fraud is committed by the company, but the purchases or sales are made by investors trading on a national securities exchange. In other words, the link or nexus between the fraud and the purchase or sale is attenuated. But that's not fatal. As long as the false or misleading statement was made in a manner that's "reasonably calculated to influence the investing public," the in connection with element is met. *See* SEC v. Texas Gulf Sulphur Co., 401 F.2d 833 (2d Cir. 1968). Statements made in a company's SEC filings certainly meet this standard. And so do statements issued in press releases, made in business or financial media, or posted on a company website or its social media accounts.

4. *Scienter*

Scienter refers to the defendant's state of mind. Specifically, it refers to a bad mental state, one involving an intent to deceive. *See* Ernst & Ernst v. Hochfelder, 425 U.S. 185 (1976). Certainly, a defendant who intentionally or knowingly misleads investors has acted with scienter. But so does a defendant who recklessly misleads investors.

What does "reckless" mean? Recklessness is much worse than unreasonableness, which is negligence standard. A common articulation of recklessness is "[h]ighly unreasonable conduct that involves an extreme departure from the standards of ordinary care, presenting a danger of misleading investors that is so obvious that the defendant must have been aware of it." *See* Webb v. SolarCity Corp., 884 F.3d 844, 851 (9th Cir. 2018). The plaintiff will have to show a level of carelessness about misleading investors that approaches indifference.

As we'll see below, the federal securities have adopted special rules that make it very difficult for plaintiffs to successfully plead scienter.

5. *Transaction Causation/Reliance*

Transaction causation is "but for" causation—but for the false or misleading statement of material fact, the investor wouldn't have purchased (or sold) the securities. Most experts use the terms "transaction causation" and "reliance" interchangeably.

If each investor in a fraud-on-the-market case were required to establish transaction causation, the federal court would be unable to certify the class action. That's because the individual questions of law or fact—whether the investor relied on the false statement—would predominate over the common questions of law or fact. To address this, the Supreme Court created a presumption of reliance that can be used in fraud-on-the-market cases. *See* Basic, Inc. v. Levinson, 485 U.S. 224 (1988).

Under this presumption, reliance is presumed if the false or misleading statement was material and the stock traded on an efficient market. The New York Stock Exchange and Nasdaq are considered to be efficient markets, which means that the fraud-on-the-market presumption of reliance applies in most securities fraud class actions.

The presumption is based on the efficient market hypothesis, which theorizes that in an efficient market, the stock price reflects all publicly available information about the company. If that's the case, the market price will also reflect the false or misleading statement. Investors purchasing (or selling) at the market price during the class period are effectively relying on the false or misleading statement. In essence, it's a form of indirect reliance: the investor relied on the price that was impacted by the false or misleading statement.

The presumption can be rebutted if the defendant can show that the market price wasn't effected by the false or misleading statement—*i.e.*, there was no "price impact." To do this, the defendant will have to present event studies prepared by experts showing, for example, that there weren't any statistically significant changes in the stock price when the false or misleading statements were made or that any changes were attributable to something other than the false or misleading statement.

In addition, the presumption can also be rebutted if the defendant can show that the plaintiff would have purchased (or sold) regardless of the false or misleading statement. For example, the defendant might be able to show that the plaintiff had business reasons to purchase the stock and would have purchased it even if the investors had been aware of the fraud.

6. Loss Causation

Loss causation is proximate causation. Was the false or misleading statement responsible for the plaintiff's losses or was something else responsible? For example, maybe the company's stock price fell not because of the fraud but because the whole stock market was down. Or maybe the plaintiff's losses were caused by other bad news that caused the company's stock price to fall.

In fraud-on-the-market class actions, the plaintiff can't plead loss causation by showing that the company's stock price was artificially inflated by the false or misleading statement. Instead, the plaintiff must show that the company's stock price fell "after the truth became known." *See* Dura Pharmaceuticals, Inc. v. Broudo, 544 U.S. 336 (2005).

There are two ways for plaintiffs to meet this standard: (1) corrective disclosure; and (2) materialization of the risk.

Under the corrective disclosure approach, the plaintiff must identify a disclosure that allegedly revealed the truth of the company's false or misleading statement and then show that the company's stock price dropped after this corrective disclosure was made.

"Corrective disclosure" could be an actual admission by the company that it had made a false or misleading statement, such as an announcement that it has restated its financial statements. Often, however, the company doesn't make an admission. In these cases, the plaintiff might point to a company's disclosure that, according to the plaintiff, revealed that the company's previous statements were false or misleading. Corrective disclosure doesn't have to be made by the company. It also includes whistleblower statements, questions by analysts, and media articles—any public disclosure where "the truth came out."

But what happens if the plaintiff can't identify a corrective disclosure? Or if the stock price didn't decline after a corrective disclosure was made? Here, the corrective disclosure approach won't work. In this case, some courts will allow the plaintiff to show loss causation through the materialization of the risk approach to loss causation.

Materialization of the risk is based on the understanding that a company's false or misleading statement subjects investors to risks that they didn't know about and wouldn't have accepted. If those risks actually occur—*i.e.*, materialize—and cause the investors to lose money, they should be able to recover those losses. Thus, in most jurisdictions, a plaintiff can plead loss causation by identifying an event or events that caused the truth about the risk to come to light and then showing that the stock price dropped after the risk materialized.

For example, assume that a company concealed that it was having serious cash flow problems. What event or events might show that the company was experiencing a liquidity crisis? Obviously, filing for bankruptcy would reveal that risk. So could a ratings downgrade by a credit rating agency. In addition, certain actions taken by the company that showed that the company needed to raise cash fast, such as selling assets or selling stock, could be seen as revealing the risk of a liquidity crisis. If the company's stock fell after one of these events, the plaintiff will be able to plead loss causation under the materialization of the risk approach.

7. Damages

Most securities fraud class action suits settle, so there's not much law on calculating damages. We do know that should be calculated on an out-of-pocket basis. That means that the plaintiff should receive the difference between what was paid for the stock and what the stock was actually worth. In other words, if the purchase price was $30, but, because of the fraud, it was only worth $20 per share on the date of purchase, the damages would be $10 per share.

That sounds easy enough, right? Unfortunately, it's not, at least not in fraud-on-the-market cases. Stock trades at different prices throughout the class period, and investors purchase it at different prices. In class actions, the trick is to find out how much the false or misleading statement artificially inflated the stock price. The starting point is the drop in stock price after the truth about the fraud comes out. So, for example, if the stock was trading at $30 per share, but then dropped to $20 per share after corrective disclosure, then the fraud presumably inflated the stock price by $10 per share. That means that all members of the class overpaid by $10 per share.

But that's just the first step. The plaintiffs and defendants then spend a lot of money on experts who run event studies trying to figure out if the value of the fraud was really $10 per share. The plaintiffs might believe that it's more than $10 per share, arguing, for example, that the company's corrective disclosure mixed positive news in with negative news, diluting the drop in stock price. On the other hand, the defendants might argue that the drop in stock price was due to a market correction that had nothing to do with the fraud.

And don't forget that some investors who purchased stock during the class period may have also sold stock during the class period. Theoretically, these "in and out" traders didn't suffer any damages. They bought at a price inflated by $10 per share, and they sold at a price inflated by $10 per share. So, in calculating the damages for the entire class, the experts have to try to figure out how many shares were purchased and sold during the class period and subtract them out of the damage award. Once again, the experts for the plaintiff and defendants will no doubt have very different ideas.

In any case, the damage award for a securities fraud class action could be crushing for a defendant. No doubt that's one of the main reasons why these actions typically settle.

8. Standing

Only investors who purchased (or sold) have standing to bring actions under Rule 10b-5. This means that investors who were defrauded into not purchasing (or not selling) securities can't bring a securities fraud claim. This group includes existing stockholders who were defrauded into holding their securities, so-called "holder claims."

D. Special Procedural Rules for Securities Fraud Class Actions

Fraud-on-the-market class actions tend to bring out strong feelings in people. Some people are big fans. They point out that class actions are necessary to deter wrongful conduct. If investors weren't allowed to sue, only the SEC would be able to enforce Rule 10b-5. Unfortunately, the SEC doesn't have enough resources to sue every public company that commits securities fraud. Recognizing that they might get away with it, unscrupulous public companies would be more likely to commit securities fraud. To prevent this, the argument goes, investors need to sue. Moreover, class actions are necessary to compensate investors for their losses.

On the other hand, there are a lot of very vocal critics who argue that many fraud-on-the-market class actions are meritless. They're brought by lawyers when there's no evidence of fraud, only an unexplained drop in stock price. According to this argument, the lawyers are using the class action to essentially extort a settlement from innocent companies. Even innocent companies will decide to settle just to make the nuisance case go away. Otherwise, they'll be subject to the costs of discovery and bad publicity, and the possibility of having to pay a huge damages award. In addition, the risk of being hit with a "strike suit" discourages companies from making voluntary disclosures in the first place. Chilling disclosure isn't good for investors. Moreover, critics point out that investors aren't adequately compensated by class actions because settlements are usually for pennies on the dollar. Their lawyers, though, make out very well, generally taking 30% or more off the top of the settlement amount. Finally, since insurance companies, not the wrongdoers, pay the settlements, critics note that class actions don't actually deter wrongful conduct.

Both sides have valid points. Sometimes we're in a pro-securities fraud class action environment, and sometimes, we're in an anti-securities fraud class action environment. The year 1995 was a very, very, VERY anti-securities fraud class action environment. Executives of public companies, especially Silicon Valley tech companies with volatile stock prices, complained to Congress about these class actions. Congress responded by enacting the Private Securities Litigation Reform Act of 1995 (PSLRA).

1. The Private Securities Litigation Reform Act of 1995

The PSLRA imposed a variety of special procedural rules that apply only to securities fraud class actions filed in federal court. The whole point of the PSLRA was to make it more difficult for plaintiffs to bring frivolous fraud-on-the-market class actions. Here's a summary of the most important provisions in the PSLRA:

Automatic Stay of Discovery. With very limited exceptions, the PSLRA imposes an automatic stay of discovery that kicks in when the defendant files a motion to dismiss. *See* Securities Exchange Act of 1934 § 21D(b)(3)(b). This means that when the defendant makes a motion to dismiss, all discovery is automatically cut off. With no discovery, the plaintiff will have a much harder time defeating the motion to dismiss—especially with the PSLRA's heightened pleading standards.

Heightened Pleading Standards. The PSLRA includes two heightened pleading standards. First, the complaint must identify each statement that's alleged to be false or misleading and must explain why it's false or misleading. In addition, plaintiffs can't simply say that these allegations are based on "information and belief." Instead, the plaintiff is required to state "with particularity" the facts supporting their belief. *See* Securities Exchange Act of 1934 § 21D(b)(1).

Second, in pleading scienter, the plaintiff must state "with particularity" facts giving rise to a "strong inference" that the defendant acted with scienter. *See* Securities Exchange Act of 1934 § 21D(b)(2). The strong inference standard, combined with the automatic stay of discovery, is an extremely powerful one-two punch to securities fraud class actions. Information about the mental state of company management is likely to be in the company's control, but the plaintiff won't be able to use discovery to get it. Because discovery isn't available, plaintiffs will be forced to find factual support in other ways, often by hiring private investigators to find current and former employees to act as "confidential witnesses."

It's not very often that a plaintiff has direct evidence of scienter. Instead, most plaintiffs have to rely on circumstantial evidence to support their allegations of scienter. Some common examples include:

- Suspicious stock trades by company management—when the company's officers buy company stock right before good news is disclosed or dump company stock right before bad news is disclosed
- Inconsistent disclosures—when the company's public statements are positive, but its internal documents tell a different story
- False or misleading statements relating to the company's "core operations"—when the false or misleading statement relates to the company's most important business or product, it's difficult to believe that management wouldn't be aware of the true state of affairs

What does "strong inference" mean? According to the Supreme Court, a strong inference must be "cogent," meaning persuasive or compelling. *See* Tellabs, Inc. v. Makor Issues & Rights, Ltd., 551 U.S. 308, 321 (2007).

In determining whether the plaintiff has met the "strong inference" standard, the court will also consider any competing inferences offered by the defendants. For example, assume company officers sold stock immediately before the company disclosed bad news. One logical inference is that the officers must've known that things at the company were bad when they sold.

But what if the defendants were able to show that the sales were planned long before the things got bad at the company? If that's the case, the officers' sales don't infer scienter. If there are competing inferences, the plaintiff wins if the plaintiff's inferences are "at least as compelling as any opposing inference one could draw from the facts alleged." *Id.* In other words, ties go to the plaintiff.

Lead Plaintiff and Lead Counsel Provisions. When a company surprises the investing public with bad news that caused the stock price to fall, numerous fraud-on-the-market class actions may be filed against the company. But there can be only one class action. So which class action will be recognized? Prior to the PSLRA, the rule was whoever filed the first complaint would represent the class. That meant a race to the courthouse.

Pre-PSLRA, certain law firms would be on the lookout for public companies suffering a big drop in stock price. When it happened, they'd quickly throw together a securities fraud complaint. The lawyers also had to find a shareholder who would agree to act as the class action representative but leave everything else to the lawyers—so called "professional plaintiffs." In effect, the lawyers, rather than the investors, were in charge of the case. And many public companies were sued for securities without any evidence of fraud.

The PSLRA stopped all of this. Now, the power to control the case is given to a "lead plaintiff" who in turn is empowered to select the "lead counsel." *See* Securities Exchange Act of 1934 § 21D(a)(3). The PSLRA's lead plaintiff provision was intended to stop the race to the courthouse. It was also designed to make securities fraud class actions less lawyer-driven and more investor-driven. Any shareholder who's a member of the class can apply to be the lead plaintiff. There's a rebuttable presumption the lead plaintiff will be the shareholder or group of shareholders that suffered the greatest financial loss. The court will review the applications and determine which of these applicants would do the best job. This shareholder will be appointed to be the "lead plaintiff."

The lead plaintiff then chooses the lead counsel, subject to court approval. *See* Securities Exchange Act of 1934 § 21D(a)(3)(B)(v).

Damages. The PSLRA also includes several provisions limiting the potential damages that could be awarded in securities fraud class actions. Congress hoped that these provisions would reduce a defendant's pressure to settle meritless actions.

First, to address concerns that damage award calculations were inflated because markets tend to overreact to the disclosure of bad news, the PSLRA includes a 90-day look-back provision. This provision caps damages to the difference between the price paid by the plaintiff and the stock's average trading price during the 90-day period following corrective disclosure. *See* Securities Exchange Act of 1934 § 21D(e).

In addition, the PSLRA eliminated joint and several liability (unless the court finds that the defendants knowingly violated Rule 10b-5). *See* Securities Exchange Act of 1934 § 21D(f)(2)(A). Otherwise, proportionate liability applies. *See* Securities Exchange Act of 1934 § 21D(f)(2)(B).

Safe Harbor for Forward-Looking Statements. During the hearings that led up to the PSLRA, public companies told Congress that they were so afraid of being sued when they made projections or forecasts that they decided not to make them anymore. To address this, Congress essentially adopted the bespeaks caution doctrine in the PSLRA. Under this statutory safe harbor, if a defendant allegedly made a false or misleading forward-looking statement, the defendant won't be liable if the forward-looking statement was "accompanied by meaningful cautionary statements identifying important factors that could cause actual results to differ materially from those in the forward-looking statement." *See* Securities Exchange Act of 1934 § 21E(c).

2. *The Securities Litigation Uniform Standards Act of 1998*

Because the PSLRA's reforms are primarily procedural, they apply only to class actions filed in federal district court. Since federal courts have exclusive jurisdiction over claims based on Rule 10b-5, that seemed like a perfectly fine and reasonable approach. *See* Securities Exchange Act of 1934 § 27. However, it didn't take lawyers too long to find a way around the PSLRA. They began to file class actions based on state law—such as state securities fraud statutes, common law fraud, or common law negligent misrepresentation—in state court, where the PSLRA didn't apply. This migration of what used to be federal Rule 10b-5 claims to state courts led Congress to close the loophole through the Securities Litigation Uniform Standards Act of 1998 (SLUSA).

SLUSA prohibits plaintiffs from bringing certain securities fraud class actions based on false or misleading statements under state law in state or federal court. *See* Securities Exchange Act of 1934 § 28. Essentially, SLUSA requires plaintiffs to bring securities fraud class actions as Rule 10b-5 claims in federal court, where they'll be subject to the PSLRA. If an action is brought in state court, the defendant can remove it to federal court, where the court will dismiss it. *See* Securities Exchange Act of 1934 § 28(f)(2).

SLUSA applies to only class actions involving a "covered security," which includes securities that trade on a national securities exchange.

E. Who Is Liable for Securities Fraud?

1. Primary Violators

A plaintiff in a fraud-on-the-market class action can sue primary violators: the person who "made" the false or misleading statement of material fact. That sounds easy enough, at least until you have to determine who "made" the statement. Think of a public company's earnings release. It's a team effort. The press release will be initially drafted by a group of employees from the company's finance department, investor relations department, major business divisions, and the general counsel's office. Then it will go to the CFO and CEO for their review. The company's outside auditors and attorneys will also have a chance for input. Finally, the company's audit committee will approve it for release. Who "made" this statement?

According to the Supreme Court, the primary violator is the person with "*ultimate authority* over the statement, including its content and whether and how to communicate it." *See* Janus Capital Group, Inc. v. First Derivative Traders, 564 U.S. 135 (2011). Furthermore, identifying the source of the statement—attribution—is strong evidence that the statement was made by that person.

This "ultimate authority" test means that many people involved in the creation of a false or misleading statement won't fall within the definition of primary violator. And this was by design; the Supreme Court wanted to limit the reach of Rule 10b-5 class actions.

Let's see how the "ultimate authority" test works in our press release example. The company itself will be a primary violator because the company had the ultimate authority—through the board—over the contents of the earnings release. Since the company works through its board of directors, that also means that the directors will be primary violators. Arguably, everyone else would escape liability—even if they knew the press release was misleading—because they didn't have ultimate authority over the press release. Drafting, reviewing, and revising a statement doesn't equate to "making" the statement.

In addition, they can't be sued as aiders and abettors. That's because the Supreme Court has held that there's no private right of action for aiding and abetting a Rule 10b-5 violation. *See* Central Bank of Denver v. First Interstate Bank of Denver, 511 U.S. 164, 177 (1994). In fact, *Central Bank* has been interpreted as eliminating private rights of action for all forms of second liability, including respondeat superior and conspiracy. In fact, there's only form of secondary liability that's available in private securities fraud actions: control person liability under Section 20 of the '34 Act.

2. Control Person Liability

Under Section 20, "control persons" are liable for the securities violations committed by someone else—even if they had nothing to do with the violation and even if they didn't even know about the violation. Imposing secondary liability reinforces the '34 Act's investor protection goals by extending liability to reach individuals who control the violators—and who therefore could presumably have prevented the violation from occurring in the first place.

In most jurisdictions, the plaintiff has to show that (1) someone made a false or misleading statement of material fact; and (2) the defendant controlled this primary violator. However, a few jurisdictions—including the Second Circuit—add a third element: that the defendant was a "culpable participant" in the fraud. Culpable participation is essentially a scienter requirement. The plaintiff must show that the defendant intended—recklessly or knowingly—to help the aid primary violator commit the fraud.

Section 20 includes a "good faith" defense. Specifically, the control person can escape liability if he "acted in good faith and did not directly or indirectly induce the act or acts constituting the violation." *See* Securities Exchange Act of 1934 § 20(a).

Obviously, the big issue with control person liability is determining who's a control person. It's not defined in Section 20, but the SEC has defined "control" to mean "the possession, direct or indirect, of the power to direct or cause the direction of the management and policies of a person, whether through the ownership of voting securities, by contract, or otherwise." *See* Securities Act of 1933 Rule 405.

Courts have struggled with whether the defendant must exert *actual* control over the primary violator or whether it's sufficient if the defendant had the *power* to control the primary violator. Many courts have adopted a compromise test incorporating both types of control. Under this two-part test, the potential defendant must (1) exercise actual control over the general operations of the violator; and (2) possess, but not necessarily exercise, the power to control the specific acts underlying the violation.

Although it's a highly fact-specific analysis, there are a few relatively straightforward examples of control persons. Majority stockholders are typically found to control the company. And corporate officers have been found to have control over the employees they supervise. On the other hand, while it would seem that the board of directors should be found to control the company, courts have been reluctant to find individual directors to be controlling persons. And law firms, investment banks, and management consulting firms aren't control persons because they can only advise, not direct, their clients.

F. Quick Recap

If a company made a false or misleading statement to the investing public, the company may have violated Rule 10b-5, the general anti-fraud provision of the '34 Act. The SEC can sue for violations of Rule 10b-5, and so can investors. However, private rights of action—especially when they're brought as class actions—are controversial. Proponents point out that securities fraud actions can deter misconduct and compensate victims, while critics argue that class actions are meritless strike-suits brought by law firms for settlement value.

This difference of opinion is why securities fraud class actions are treated so differently than other kinds of litigation. We see that in the PSLRA and SLUSA. And we see it private securities fraud cases. Some judges are suspicious of fraud-on-the-market cases. If the judge believes that most fraud-on-the-market cases are frivolous, the court may well adopt a pro-defendant holding. On the other hand, if a judge believes that fraud-on-the-market cases provide significant societal benefits, the judge will be more likely to adopt a pro-plaintiff holding. Judges don't hide from policy arguments; they often directly engage with policy arguments in their opinions. On an exam, so should you!

CHAPTER 12

Insider Trading

A. Introduction

Insider trading gets a lot of attention, whether it's through TV shows like "Billions" or through media coverage of high profile civil or criminal actions against wealthy Wall Street financiers. Enforcement of the insider trading rules has been one of the SEC's most important initiatives for years. Why? What's so bad about it?

Most of us don't like insider trading because it seems unfair. It just doesn't seem right that someone was able to make money because of an informational advantage, especially an advantage that's due to the person's insider status. Most of us believe that everyone should have equal access to information when they trade stock. This is sometimes referred to as a "parity of information" argument. And this leads to a second concern: that insider trading erodes investor confidence in the fairness and integrity of the securities markets. If investors believe the market is unfair, they'll take their money out of the markets. That would be a bad thing because we need investors to have strong stock markets. Thus, insider trading raises concerns about investor protection and concerns about maintaining fair, orderly, and efficient markets.

Insider trading is primarily regulated by Rule 10b-5, so that's the focus of this chapter. However, this chapter also covers other approaches to insider trading, including Rule 14e-3, short swing profits under Section 16, and Regulation FD.

B. Insider Trading and Rule 10b-5

If you were to ask a non-lawyer to define insider trading, he would probably describe it as occurring when a person with non-public information about a company buys or sells stock without disclosing that information to the person he's trading with. In other words, that there wasn't "parity of information." But that definition isn't correct. That's because insider trading is primarily regulated by Rule 10b-5(a) or (c). For insider trading to be illegal under Rule 10b-5, there has to be fraud.

It's black letter law that silence isn't fraudulent—unless the person had a duty to speak up. Put another way, merely possessing non-public information isn't fraudulent. It may be unfair, but it's not fraudulent. What makes it fraudulent is that the trade was made in violation of a duty to disclose. This is why insider trading is often referred to as a "disclose or abstain" rule. If the person with the duty doesn't disclose the information, he has to abstain from trading.

The key to insider trading, then, is identifying a duty. The Supreme Court has used five theories of insider trading to identify a duty: (1) the classical theory; (2) constructive insider theory; (3) tipper-tippee theory; (4) misappropriation theory; and (5) tipping of misappropriated information.

1. Theories of Insider Trading

Classical Theory of Insider Trading. Under the classical theory of insider trading, the defendant committed fraud if he owed a duty to disclose the information to his or her trading partner.

But where does this duty come from? Often it's derived from the person's status as an insider—such as an officer or director—of the company. As you might remember from your Business Organizations class, state corporate law imposes fiduciary duties on corporate officers and directors. These fiduciary duties require them to deal fairly with company shareholders.

The classic example of the classical theory occurs when an officer with material non-public information buys company stock on a national securities exchange. The officer's trading partner is the seller of the stock, who is necessarily an existing shareholder of the company. It doesn't matter that officer didn't know who sold the stock to him. The seller was a company shareholder, so the officer owes fiduciary duties to that person because of his status as a company officer. This means the officer has a duty to speak up and disclose the information to his trading partner. If he doesn't, his silence would be fraudulent.

This example doesn't work so well if the officer with material non-public information *sells* company stock. In this case, the officer's trading partner is the purchaser. When the sale is made on an exchange, it's impossible to know whether the officer sold to an existing shareholder. If the sale wasn't made to an existing shareholder, the purchaser would be a stranger to the officer; no fiduciary duties would be owed to him. Strangely enough, however, most courts have overlooked this distinction and have held that an officer who sells stock has a duty to his trading partner.

In addition to corporate law, there are other sources of duties under the classical theory of insider trading, including agency law and partnership law.

So when can a person with material non-public information trade under the classical theory? When he has no duty to his trading partner. This is what happened in the *Chiarella* case, which is the seminal insider trading case. *See* Chiarella v. United States, 45 U.S. 222 (1980). In that case, Chiarella, an employee of a financial printer, used the documents he was typesetting to figure out the identities of companies that were going to be taken over in hostile tender offers. After purchasing stock in these companies before the information was made public, he was convicted of insider trading. The Supreme Court reversed, expressly rejecting a "parity of information" theory of insider trading. The court noted that while Chiarella had traded on material non-public information, he had no duty to his trading partners. He wasn't a corporate insider and, in fact, had no relationship at all with the sellers. He was a stranger to them. Without a duty, there could be no fraud. Put another way, the court held that "a duty to disclose under Section 10(b) does not arise from the mere possession of nonpublic market information." *See id.*

Constructive Insider Theory of Insider Trading. We know that, under the classical theory, a company's officers and directors can't trade on the basis of material non-public information. But what if the company's investment bank does? Has it committed fraud? As we know, it depends on whether the investment bank has a duty to its trading partner.

The investment bank might argue that it didn't, that it was a stranger to its trading partner. Courts, however, have determined that advisers like the investment bank will become subject to the insider's duty if:

- The adviser has entered into a special confidential relationship with the company;
- The material non-public information was disclosed to the adviser for legitimate corporate purposes; and
- The company must have expected that the adviser would keep the information confidential.

Therefore, company advisers such as investment banks, attorneys, accountants, and consultants are generally treated as if they're insiders. Therefore, they would have a duty to their trading partners.

Tipper-Tippee Theory of Insider Trading. Sometimes, the person with the duty doesn't trade but tips someone who does trade. For example, a company officer might disclose material non-public information to a third party, who purchases stock in the company. Under the classical theory, Rule 10b-5 wouldn't be violated because the person who traded presumably didn't have a duty to his trading partner. This is where the tipper-tippee theory kicks in. If the tipper-tippee theory applies, the tippee will be found to have inherited the insider's duty.

In Dirks v. SEC, the Supreme Court set forth a two-part test. Under this test, the tippee will assume the insider's duty not to trade on material non-public information when:

1. The insider has breached his duty to the shareholders by disclosing information to the tippee; and
2. The tippee knows or should know that the insider's disclosure was a breach of duty

See Dirks v. SEC, 463 U.S. 646 (1983).

Not all disclosures by insiders to third parties constitute a breach of duty. For example, a company officer might've disclosed material non-public information to another company employee for legitimate business reasons. That disclosure isn't wrongful. For the disclosure to be a breach of duty, the insider must have disclosed to get a "personal benefit." In other words, it turns on the insider's motivation. Ask yourself, why did the insider disclose the information? If it was to gain a monetary or financial benefit, the disclosure constituted a breach.

The definition of "personal benefit" is pretty broad. It includes:

- Outright cash payments to the insider
- Future earnings to the insider from quid pro quo arrangements; *i.e.*, "I tip you this time, you tip me next time"
- Future earnings that would presumably come to the insider from using tips to boost the insider's business reputation or curry favor with important clients
- Gifts to the insider's family members and close friends; if the tip is unwound, it's as if the insider traded and then gifted the monetary profits to the recipient of the tip

While most of the action in tipper-tippee liability is in the first prong of the *Dirks* test, don't forget that there's a second prong: that the tippee knows or should know that the tipper's disclosure was a breach of duty. The purpose of this prong is to ensure that the tippee won't be held liable for insider trading simply because he was aware that he had material non-public information. Remember, mere possession of material non-public information doesn't constitute fraud.

To be held liable, the tippee must be aware that the information was given to him wrongfully. When disclosure is directly made by the tipper to the tippee, it's relatively easy to make this showing.

On the other hand, what about a person who was tipped by the initial tippee? Or someone who was tipped by the tippee of the initial tippee? And so on down the line. This is referred to as "remote tipping." The remote tippee wouldn't necessarily know the circumstances surrounding the tipper's initial disclosure or whether it was wrongful. Moreover, at some point, the information becomes divorced from the tipper; the information is more like a rumor than a tip. In these remote tipping cases, it's much harder to meet the second prong.

Misappropriation Theory of Insider Trading. While the classical, constructive insider, and tipper-tippee theories capture a lot of insider trading, they don't capture all of it. In fact, for many years, the SEC was concerned with the amount of trading that could be traced back to insiders disclosing material non-public information during conversations with family members or friends.

As we know, most people talk about their jobs—the good things and the bad things—to their family and friends. For example, let's assume that the CEO of a public company just learned that the FDA wasn't going to approve the company's new drug. The CEO was stressed out and confided in his spouse. That's what spouses often do.

But what happens if the spouse then traded on that material non-public information? The spouse wouldn't be liable under the classical theory because the spouse didn't have a duty to her trading partner. The spouse wasn't a constructive insider because the information wasn't disclosed to her for a legitimate business purpose. Finally, the spouse wouldn't have inherited the CEO's duty under the tipper-tippee theory because the insider didn't disclose the information to obtain a personal benefit; his motivation was to share his concerns with his spouse. Since the spouse had no duty to her trading partner, she could remain silent. Silence, absent a duty to disclose, does not constitute fraud.

To address this situation, the Supreme Court adopted the misappropriation theory. *See* United States v. O'Hagan, 521 U.S. 642 (1997). The court knew it had to find a duty to find the fraud necessary for a Rule 10b-5 action. Under the misappropriation theory of insider trading, the duty is to the *source* of the information, not the trading partner. That's the difference between the classical theory and the misappropriation theory. Under the classical theory, the duty is owed to the trading partner. Under the misappropriation theory, the duty is owed to the source of the information. In other words, under misappropriation theory, the source of the information is being defrauded, not the trading partner.

Where might a duty to the source of the information come from? It might come from:

- Fiduciary duty: a state's common law might impose a duty, such as agency law, partnership law, and corporate law.
- Professional duty: a person's occupation might impose a duty of confidentiality; common examples include attorneys, therapists, and religious advisers.

In addition, the SEC adopted Rule 10b5-2, which sets forth a list of duties of trust or confidence that support the misappropriation theory:

- By agreement: whenever a person agrees to keep information confidential.
- Through close friendships: whenever "the person communicating the material nonpublic information

and the person to whom it is communicated have a history, pattern, or practice of sharing confidences, such that the recipient of the information knows or reasonably should know that the person communicating the material nonpublic information expects that the recipient will maintain its confidentiality."

- Through certain family relationships: Whenever "a person receives or obtains material nonpublic information from his or her spouse, parent, child, or sibling." However, this presumption of duty can be rebutted if the defendant can show that no duty of trust of confidence actually existed between the family members.

The misappropriation theory is a game changer. Its reach is extremely broad. It reaches the CEO's spouse in our earlier hypothetical. According to Rule 10b5-2, she owes a duty of trust to her husband. When she traded on the information he disclosed to her, she defrauded him.

Tipping of Misappropriated Information Theory of Insider Trading. Sometimes a person misappropriates information but doesn't trade on it. Instead, the person discloses the misappropriated information to someone else who trades. For example, let's continue working with our hypo about the CEO who disclosed material non-public information to his wife because he was stressed out. This time, his wife didn't trade on the information, but she disclosed the information to someone else for a payment of $10,000. Did the person who traded violate Rule 10b-5? As always, it depends on whether the trader had a duty.

At first glance, it doesn't look good. Let's go through each theory. First, the trader doesn't have a duty to his trading partner; he's a stranger to them. So the classical theory doesn't work.

Second, the trader isn't a constructive insider because the company didn't provide this information to the trader for legitimate business reasons. Third, the trader didn't inherit the CEO's duty under the tipper-tippee theory. Note that the wife never inherited her husband's duty because the insider didn't disclose the information to her to receive personal benefit. If the wife didn't inherit the husband's duty under the tipper-tippee theory, she can't pass it on to the trader. And, fourth, the trader didn't misappropriate the information from the wife. The trader didn't agree to keep the information confidential or not trade on it, and the trader wasn't a family member or friend. On the contrary, the wife was well aware that the trader was going to trade on the material non-public information. That's why she charged $10,000 for it.

So this leaves the final theory, which combines tipper-tippee liability with the misappropriation theory. We know that Rule 10b5-2 imposes a duty of trust on the wife. That means she can't trade on information she received from her husband. It also means she can't disclose it to anyone else. When she tipped the trader, the trader might have inherited her duty to her spouse. We need a mashup of the misappropriation theory and the *Dirks* test for tipper-tippee liability. To do this, the word "insider" should be replaced with "misappropriator," and the word "shareholders" should be replaced with "source."

Under this modified test, the tippee will assume the ~~insider's~~ **misappropriator's** duty not to trade on material non-public information when:

1. The ~~insider~~ **misappropriator** has breached his duty to the ~~shareholders~~ **source** by disclosing information to the tippee; and

2. The tippee knows or should know that the ~~insider's~~ **misappropriator's** disclosure was a breach of duty

In our hypothetical, the first prong is met because the wife (the misappropriator) received a personal benefit (the $10,000 payment) for the tip. Therefore, the trader inherited her duty. The second prong is met because the $10,000 payment is strong evidence that the trader knew that the wife improperly disclosed the material non-public information to him.

2. Elements of an Insider Trading Violation

Insider trading occurs when (1) a person trades (2) on the basis of (3) material non-public information (4) in breach of a duty. In addition, the defendant must have acted with scienter. The elements are discussed in more detail below.

A Person Trades. Obviously, there's no insider trading unless someone trades.

"On the Basis Of". The "on the basis" of element is essentially a causation element. It provides the link between the material non-public information and the trading decision. Initially, courts were split on the meaning of "on the basis of." Some courts required that the trader had to *use* the non-public information; *i.e.*, that he traded because of the material non-public information. Other courts merely required that the trader was *aware* of the material non-public information at the time of the transaction. These courts presumed that someone with material non-public information would use it.

Why does it make a difference? Think of an insider who had already made plans to sell company stock before he learned about the material non-public information. Courts following the "awareness" approach would find that he traded on the basis of the material non-public information. On the other hand, courts following the "use" approach would find that this element wasn't met because he was going to sell the stock regardless of the material non-public information.

Nowadays, the issue is settled by SEC rulemaking. In Rule 10b5-1, the SEC compromised. Rule 10b5-1 adopts the awareness approach. However, it also provides an affirmative defense for defendants who can show that they didn't use the information because, before they became aware of the material non-public information, they (1) entered into a contract to buy or sell the stock; (2) instructed someone to buy or sell the stock; or (3) adopted a so-called Rule 10b5-1 trading plan.

A Rule 10b5-1 trading plan provides for pre-planned purchases or sales of company securities. For example, the insider might want to sell company stock to diversify his investments. In this case, the plan might provide that each month 5,000 shares of company stock will be sold at $100 per share or better. Because the transactions were planned before the defendants became aware of the material non-public information, the defendants didn't use the information when the transaction occurred.

Rule 10b5-1 sets forth several requirements for trading plans, including that the plan specify the amount of stock, the price, and the date on which the stock will be purchased or sold. Not surprising, the insider can't exercise any discretion over the trading plan. In addition, for company officers and directors, there's a "cooling off" period. In general, trades can't occur under the trading plan until 90 days after the trading plan was adopted.

The Rule 10b5-1 trading plan is how most insiders are able to buy or sell stock without violating the insider trading rules.

Material Non-public Information. Information is material if there's a substantial likelihood that a reasonable investor would find it important in deciding how to act. For more discussion of materiality, see Chapter 11.

Non-public information means information that hasn't been broadly disseminated to the public. For information to be public, it needs to be disclosed in a press release, in a document filed with the SEC (such as a Form 8-K), or through a posting on the company's website or social media. In addition, there must be enough time for information to reach the investing public. That means, for example, that an insider can't trade right after a press release is issued. The insider will have to wait until the market has had enough time to read and understand the significance of the information. Most experts advise waiting at least two business days after the disclosure.

In Breach of a Duty. Trading in breach of a duty turns the silence into fraud. As we know from the above section, the key to insider trading liability is finding the duty.

Scienter. Just like any other claim based on Rule 10b-5, the defendant has to have acted with scienter. For insider trading claims, that means that that the defendant knowingly traded on the basis on material non-public information or was reckless in not knowing that he was trading on the basis of material non-public information.

C. Rule 14e-3

The SEC has always been especially concerned with insider trading involving takeovers. That's because it's an especially fertile ground for insider trading. Just think of the amount of money someone could make if they bought stock in a target company before the tender offer was launched. In fact, that's what happened in the *Chiarella* case discussed above.

The SEC wasn't happy with the Supreme Court's decision in *Chiarella*. Remember, in that case, the Supreme Court held that fraud under Rule 10b-5 could occur only if the person trading had a duty to his trading partner. In doing so, it rejected the SEC's argument that trading while in possession of material non-public information should be a violation of Rule 10b-5.

It didn't take the SEC long to respond. Several months after *Chiarella*, the SEC adopted Rule 14e-3, which prohibits anyone *in possession* of material non-public information relating to a tender offer from trading in the target company's securities. In other words, it doesn't require a breach of a duty. Rule 14e-3 kicks in when the bidder has taken a "substantial step" towards launching a tender offer.

Note that the SEC was able to get around the *Chiarella* decision by relying on Section 14(e)—which prohibits fraud in connection with tender offers—to adopt the rule. Not surprisingly, the SEC was accused of exceeding its rulemaking authority under Section 14(e) when it adopted Rule 14e-3. However, the Supreme Court upheld the validity of Rule 14e-3, noting that Section 14(e) included language authorizing the SEC not just to adopt rules prohibiting fraud in tender offers but to adopt rules that are "reasonably designed to prevent" fraud in tender offers. *See* United States v. O'Hagan, 521 U.S. 642 (1997).

D. Section 16

While Rule 10b-5 does most of the heavy lifting in insider trading, Section 16 also has a role. Section 16 is known as the "short swing profits" rule. It requires certain insiders—company officers, directors, and 10% shareholders—to disgorge to the company any profits made by buying and selling company securities within a six-month period. Section 16 is premised on the idea that purchases and sales made within such a short period of time by company insiders are presumably motivated by material non-public information.

How does Section 16 work? Let's assume that a director purchased 1,000 shares of stock of company stock on March 2nd at

$15 per share. Then the director sold 1,000 shares of stock on April 13th at $20 per share. The director made a profit of $5 per share in the sale. If a Section 16 action is brought against the director, she must disgorge her profits of $10 per share for a total of $5,000.

This seems relatively straightforward, right? Well, it's much more complicated. To give Section 16 maximum effect, the courts match the highest sales price with the lowest purchase price in any six-month period, regardless of the order of transactions. For example, let's assume that a director sold 1,000 shares of company stock on January 15th at $25 per share. Then the director purchased 1,000 shares of company stock on March 2nd at $15 per share. Finally, the director sold 1,000 shares of company stock on April 13th at $20 per share. In this example, the highest sales price was $25 per share and the lowest purchase price was $15 per share. That means that a profit of $10 per share must be disgorged—even though the sale occurred before the purchase.

To facilitate Section 16, officers, directors, and 10% shareholders are required to file reports with the SEC when they buy and sell stock in their company. There are three disclosure forms:

- Form 3: the report that initially discloses the insider's ownership of company stock; it must be filed within 10 days of becoming a company insider
- Form 4: the report that discloses the insider's purchases or sales in company securities; it must be filed within two days of the transaction
- Form 5: an annual report which must disclose any transactions that weren't disclosed in Form 4 filings; it must be filed within 45 days of the end of the company's fiscal year

E. Regulation FD

The goal of Regulation FD (Fair Disclosure) is to provide investors with equal access to material information. It does this by prohibiting public companies from sharing material information privately with analysts and institutional investors before disclosing the information to the public.

Prior to Regulation FD, it was common for public companies to disclose important information to market professionals, such as analysts, without disclosing the same information to the public. This often occurred when a public company believed that analyst projections of company earnings were too high. Company executives knew that if the projections weren't corrected, Wall Street would be surprised when the company ultimately disclosed its disappointing quarterly earnings—and that's never a good thing for the company's stock price. To prevent this, company management would call the analysts and encourage them to adjust their guidance. This selective disclosure of material non-public information clearly gave an unfair advantage to market professionals over retail investors.

Regulation FD prohibits this practice. Companies aren't allowed to provide earnings guidance or any other material non-public information to market professionals (analysts and institutional investors) unless the information is simultaneously provided to the public. Regulation FD makes clear that only the SEC can enforce the rule. There's no private right of action for violations of the rule.

To determine if Regulation FD has been violated, you should ask:

- Is the disclosing employee covered by the rule?
- Is the information material non-public information?

- Was disclosure made to a covered person?
- Was public disclosure made in a timely manner?

Disclosing Employee. Regulation FD regulates disclosures only by certain company employees. Specifically, it applies to the issuer and "persons acting on behalf of the issuer." That includes the company's directors, executive officers, investor relations office, as well as any other employee who "regularly communicates" with market professionals. No one else can subject the company to liability under Regulation FD, unless they were directed to disclose the information by one of the employees who's covered by the rule.

Material Non-Public Information. The non-public information must be material. It's the same test that's used throughout the federal securities laws: whether there's a substantial likelihood that a reasonable investor would consider the information important in deciding how to act. When it adopted Regulation FD, the SEC identified certain categories of information as being material, including earnings guidance, mergers and acquisitions, new product announcements, management changes, and events related to the company's stock (such as dividend policy and stock splits).

Covered Person. Regulation FD only applies to disclosures made outside the company to certain market professionals such as brokers, investment advisors, analysts, and institutional investors.

Timeliness of Public Disclosure. Whether the public disclosure was timely depends on whether the private disclosure was "intentional" or "non-intentional."

If a company intentionally provided material non-public information to market professionals, the company has violated Regulation FD.

On the other hand, if the company negligently disclosed material non-public information to market professionals, the public company can avoid violating Regulation FD. The public company must disclose the information to the public "promptly" after a senior officer of the public company becomes aware of the selective disclosure. Promptly means within 24 hours.

Public disclosure can be made in several ways, including by issuing a press release, by filing a Form 8-K, or by posting on the company's website or social media (assuming the company uses its website or social media to disclose information to the public). Companies can also use teleconferences. For example, many public companies host their earnings calls with analysts through teleconferences open to all investors, who are permitted to listen to the presentation and conversation (but not ask questions).

F. Quick Recap

Insider trading isn't "I know something you don't know." Insider trading is primarily regulated through Rule 10b-5, and that requires fraud. Silence, absent a duty to disclose, isn't fraud. So if you get an insider trading question on your exam, you need to identify the duty. And remember that there might be more than one duty. That's because the misappropriation theory captures many forms of insider trading.

The unfairness inherent in insider trading is addressed in other rules, such as Rule 14e-3, which prohibits trading while in possession of material non-public information relating to a tender offer, and Regulation FD, which prohibits certain types of selective disclosure.